WHAT THE BIBLE SAYS ABOUT DEALING WITH YOUR EMOTIONS

BY CRISWELL FREEMAN

SMITH FREEMAN Publishing

What the Bible Says about Dealing with Your Emotions
by Criswell Freeman

©2021 Smith Freeman Publishing

Bible verses were taken from the following translations:

Scripture quotations marked HCSB are taken from the Holman Christian Standard Bible®, Used by Permission HCSB © 1999, 2000, 2002, 2003, 2009 Holman Bible Publishers. Holman Christian Standard Bible®, Holman CSB®, and HCSB® are federally registered trademarks of Holman Bible Publishers.

Scripture quotations marked KJV are from the King James Version. Public domain.

Scripture quotations marked MSG are taken from THE MESSAGE, copyright © 1993, 2002, 2018 by Eugene H. Peterson. Used by permission of NavPress. All rights reserved. Represented by Tyndale House Publishers, a Division of Tyndale House Ministries.

Scripture quotations marked NASB are from the New American Standard Bible® (NASB), Copyright © 1960, 1962, 1963,1968, 1971, 1972, 1973, 1975, 1977, 1995 by The Lockman Foundation. Used by permission. www.Lockman.org.

Scripture quotations marked NCV are taken from the New Century Version®. Copyright © 2005 by Thomas Nelson. Used by permission. All rights reserved.

Scripture quotations marked NIV are taken from the Holy Bible, New International Version®, NIV®. Copyright © 1973, 1978, 1984, 2011 by Biblica, Inc.™ Used by permission of Zondervan. All rights reserved worldwide. www.zondervan.com The "NIV" and "New International Version" are trademarks registered in the United States Patent and Trademark Office by Biblica, Inc.™

Scripture quotations marked NKJV are taken from the New King James Version®. Copyright © 1982 by Thomas Nelson. Used by permission. All rights reserved.

Scripture quotations marked NLT are taken from the Holy Bible, New Living Translation, copyright © 1996, 2004, 2015 by Tyndale House Foundation. Used by permission of Tyndale House Publishers, a Division of Tyndale House Ministries, Carol Stream, Illinois 60188. All rights reserved.

Cover design by Kim Russell | Wahoo Designs

ISBN: 978-1-7349737-7-8

Contents

A Message to Readers 5
Seven Steps for Dealing with Your Emotions 6

1 Emotional Ups and Downs Are a Fact of Life 8
2 When You Ask God for Help to Control
   Your Emotions, He Will Respond 11
3 Negative Emotions Can Be Dangerous,
   Destructive, and Counterproductive 14
4 Understanding Depression 17
5 God Will Help You Manage Anxiety 20
6 A Morning Devotional Will Help You
   Prepare for the Day Ahead 23
7 Maintain the Right Kind of Attitude 26
8 Treating PTSD 29
9 Emotions Are Contagious 31
10 Impulsivity Can Be Hazardous to
   Your Emotional Health 33
11 Chronic Negativity Is an Emotional Dead End 36
12 God Will Help You Deal with Change 39
13 With God's Help, You Can Learn to
   Deal with Difficult People 42
14 God Wants You to Live Abundantly 45
15 God Doesn't Intend for You to
   Burn Out Physically or Emotionally 48
16 It's Wise to Avoid Dead-End Arguments 51
17 Draw Confidence from God 54

18	When You Grieve, the Lord Offers Comfort	57
19	Failure Isn't Final	60
20	Beware of Bitterness	63
21	You Can Learn to Control Anger Before It Controls You	66
22	Navigating Difficult Relationships	69
23	When Your Heart Is Troubled, Have Courage	72
24	Guard Your Heart	75
25	Don't Panic!	78
26	You Can Free Yourself from the Pain of Perfectionism	81
27	Beyond Shame	84
28	To Maintain Emotional Stability, It Often Helps to Establish Boundaries	87
29	You Can Take Your Worries to God and Leave Them There	90
30	Beyond Procrastination	92
31	Don't Play the Blame Game	95
32	Fear Not; God Is Bigger Than Your Difficulties	98
33	Say No to Chronic Complaining	101
34	God Wants You to Forgive Everybody, Including Yourself	104
35	Too Edgy?	107
36	If You're Starting Over	110
37	When You're Suffering, God Can Heal You	113
38	Trust God's Wisdom	116
39	Stay Focused on God's Gift of Eternal Life	118

Common Mood and Anxiety Disorders 121

A MESSAGE TO READERS

We relish our positive emotions and dread the counterproductive ones. Given our choice, we would spend all our days feeling joyful, peaceful, grateful, and contented. And we'd waste no time dealing with unfounded anxieties and needless negativity. But life doesn't always work that way. Sometimes we're attacked by negative emotions that darken our thoughts and harden our hearts.

God wants you to guard your heart against negative emotions and the destructive behaviors that result from them, so He has given you a guidebook for spiritual, emotional, physical, and psychological health. That book, of course, is the Holy Bible. The Bible is a priceless gift, an infallible tool that God intends for you to use every day, in good times and in hard times. Your intentions should be the same.

If you sometimes feel like you're on an emotional roller coaster—or if you're plagued by negative emotions that leave you feeling angry, disheartened, or despondent—the ideas in this book will provide the wisdom, the courage, and the practical advice you'll need to manage your thoughts and improve your outlook.

When you weave God's message into the fabric of your day, you'll quickly discover that God's Word has the power to change everything, including your outlook, your attitude, and your responses. So if you sincerely desire to find better strategies for dealing with the emotional ups and downs of everyday life, don't give up. Instead, keep searching for direction—God's direction. When you do, you'll discover the comfort, the power, the wisdom, and the peace that only He can give.

SEVEN STEPS FOR DEALING WITH YOUR EMOTIONS

I have come that they may have life, and that they may have it more abundantly.
John 10:10 NKJV

Accept the Fact That Negative Emotions Are Dangerous to Your Mental, Spiritual, and Physical Health. God wants you to experience the abundant life that He describes in John 10:10. To achieve it, you must guard your heart against negative emotions and the destructive behaviors that negative emotions inevitably cause.

Recognize That It's Possible to Exert Control Over Your Emotions. If you believe that you have no control over your emotions, you're wrong. It may take training, education, and practice, but if you sincerely desire to gain better control over your emotions, you can do it. With God, all things are possible.

Identify Any Chronic Negative Feelings and Turn Them Over to God. Make no room in your heart for anger, regret, bitterness, envy, or any other negative emotion that threatens your sanity and steals your joy.

Understand That Emotions Are Highly Contagious. Unless you make the conscious effort to take control of your thoughts and emotions, other people's emotions can hijack yours.

Forgive Everybody. It's God's rule, and it should be your rule too. The sooner you forgive, the sooner you'll begin feeling better about yourself and your world.

When You Experience a Significant Loss, Express Your Feelings Honestly. If you're experiencing tough times or recovering from a tragic loss, don't keep everything bottled up inside. Express your feelings, and while you're at it, remember that God promises to heal the brokenhearted. In time, He will dry your tears if you let Him. And if you haven't already allowed Him to begin His healing process, today is the perfect day to start.

If Your Emotions—or the Emotions of Someone You Love—Begin to Spiral Out of Control, Seek Professional Help Immediately. Small emotional swings are an inevitable part of life. But dramatic emotional swings—either extreme, unrelenting sadness or manic symptoms such as grandiose thinking or intense irritability—can be dangerous. So don't be embarrassed to seek professional guidance. Mental health professionals have numerous tools to help you deal with emotional swings and mood disorders. Since help is available, you should ask for it.

1

EMOTIONAL UPS AND DOWNS ARE A FACT OF LIFE

What the Bible Says

Should we accept only good things from the hand of God and never anything bad?

JOB 2:10 NLT

From time to time, all of us experience emotional swings. Even the most even-tempered among us experience natural human emotions such as anger, sadness, anxiety, and fear. Since we cannot eliminate these emotional highs and lows, we should seek to understand them. And we should learn to control our negative emotions before they take control of us.

When you encounter unfortunate circumstances that you cannot change, here's a proven way to retain your sanity: accept those circumstances (no matter how unpleasant), and trust God. The American theologian Reinhold Niebuhr composed a profoundly simple verse that came to be known as the Serenity Prayer: "God, grant me the serenity to accept the things I cannot change, the courage to change the things I can, and the wisdom to know the difference." Niebuhr's words are far easier to recite than they are to live by. Why? Because most of us want life to unfold in accordance with our own wishes and timetables. But sometimes God has other plans.

When you trust God completely and without reservation, you'll soon discover that your emotional swings will be less dramatic and less painful. Then you can be comforted in the knowledge that your Creator is both loving and wise, and that He understands His plans perfectly, even when you do not.

MORE THOUGHTS ABOUT EMOTIONS

Our emotions can lie to us, and we need to counter our emotions with truth.
BILLY GRAHAM

It is Christ who is to be exalted, not our feelings. We will know Him by obedience, not by emotions. Our love will be shown by obedience, not by how good we feel about God at a given moment.
ELISABETH ELLIOT

If you desire to improve your physical well-being and your emotional outlook, increasing your faith can help you.
JOHN MAXWELL

Faith is the art of holding on to things your reason has once accepted in spite of your changing moods.
C. S. LEWIS

The truth is that even in the midst of trouble, happy moments swim by us every day, like shining fish waiting to be caught.
BARBARA JOHNSON

MORE FROM GOD'S WORD

For this very reason, make every effort to supplement your faith with goodness, goodness with knowledge, knowledge with self-control, self-control with endurance, endurance with godliness.
2 PETER 1:5–6 HCSB

To do evil is like sport to a fool, but a man of understanding has wisdom.
PROVERBS 10:23 NKJV

Get wisdom—how much better it is than gold! And get understanding—it is preferable to silver.
PROVERBS 16:16 HCSB

REMEMBER THIS

Emotional ups and downs are an inevitable part of life. So if you're feeling anxious, worried, or afraid, remember that those feelings, like all human emotions, will pass. And they will pass more quickly if you ask God to help you spend more time solving problems and less time fretting over them.

A TIMELY TIP

If you're experiencing hurtful feelings that just won't go away, it's time to schedule an appointment with your pastor or a pastoral counselor or with your physician or a mental health professional. These people can help you look inside to discover, and then to banish, the hurtful feelings or exaggerated thought patterns that may be holding you back.

2

WHEN YOU ASK GOD FOR HELP TO CONTROL YOUR EMOTIONS, HE WILL RESPOND

What the Bible Says

Ask, and it will be given to you; seek, and you will find; knock, and it will be opened to you. For everyone who asks receives, and the one who seeks finds, and to the one who knocks it will be opened.

MATTHEW 7:7–8 NASB

If you're dealing with roller-coaster emotions, you need God's help. And if you ask Him, He will most certainly provide the help you need. So how often do you ask God for His help and His wisdom? Occasionally? Intermittently? Whenever you experience a crisis? Hopefully not. Hopefully you've acquired the habit of asking for God's assistance early and often. And hopefully you have learned to seek His guidance in every aspect of your life.

Jesus made it clear to His disciples: They should petition God to meet their needs. So should you. Genuine, heartfelt prayer produces powerful changes in you and in your world. God can do great things through you if you have the courage to ask Him (and the determination to keep asking Him). But don't expect Him to do all the work. When you do your part, He will do His part; when He does, you can expect miracles to happen.

The Bible promises that God will guide you if you let Him. Your job is to let Him. When you ask for His help, He will not withhold it. So ask. Ask Him to meet the needs of your day. Ask Him to lead you, to protect you, and to correct you. Then trust the answers He gives.

The Lord stands at the door and waits. When you knock, He opens. When you ask, He answers. Your task, of course, is to make God a full partner in every aspect of your life and to seek His guidance prayerfully, confidently, and often.

MORE THOUGHTS ABOUT ASKING GOD FOR THE THINGS YOU NEED

Are you serious about wanting God's guidance to become a personal reality in your life? The first step is to tell God that you know you can't manage your own life; that you need His help.

CATHERINE MARSHALL

God will help us become the people we are meant to be, if only we will ask Him.

HANNAH WHITALL SMITH

God insists that we ask, not because He needs to know our situation, but because we need the spiritual discipline of asking.

CATHERINE MARSHALL

When you ask God to do something, don't ask timidly; put your whole heart into it.

MARIE T. FREEMAN

MORE FROM GOD'S WORD

You did not choose me, but I chose you and appointed you so that you might go and bear fruit—fruit that will last—and so that whatever you ask in my name the Father will give you.

JOHN 15:16 NIV

Do not be anxious about anything, but in every situation, by prayer and petition, with thanksgiving, present your requests to God.

PHILIPPIANS 4:6 NIV

Your Father knows the things you have need of before you ask Him.

MATTHEW 6:8 NKJV

REMEMBER THIS

If you're having trouble dealing with your emotions, ask for God's help. And remember that if you have questions, God has answers. So when in doubt, pray. And keep praying until the answers arrive.

A TIMELY TIP

Think of a specific need that is weighing heavily on your heart. Then spend a few moments each day asking God for His guidance and for His help. When you ask, He will answer in His own time and in His own way.

3

NEGATIVE EMOTIONS CAN BE DANGEROUS, DESTRUCTIVE, AND COUNTERPRODUCTIVE

What the Bible Says

All bitterness, anger and wrath, shouting and slander must be removed from you, along with all malice. And be kind and compassionate to one another, forgiving one another, just as God also forgave you in Christ.

EPHESIANS 4:31–32 HCSB

Time and again, the Bible instructs us to trust God so that we might experience the peace that He offers to those who follow in the footsteps of His only begotten Son. Yet despite our best intentions, negative feelings can rob us of the peace and abundance that could—and should—be ours through Christ. When anger, frustration, impatience, or anxiety separates us from the spiritual blessings that the Lord has in store, we must rethink our priorities. And we must place faith above feelings.

Human emotions are highly variable, decidedly unpredictable, and often unreliable. Our emotions change like the weather, but sometimes they're even less predictable, and far more fickle, than the local weather forecast. So we must learn to live by faith, not by the ups and downs of our own emotional roller coasters.

Who's pulling your emotional strings? Are you allowing highly emotional people or highly charged situations to dictate your moods, or are you wiser than that? Sometime during the coming day, you may encounter a tough situation or a difficult person. And as a result, you may be gripped by a strong negative emotion. Distrust it. Rein it in. Test it. And turn it over to the Lord.

Your emotions will inevitably change; God will not. So trust Him completely. When you do, you'll be surprised at how quickly those negative feelings will evaporate into thin air.

MORE THOUGHTS ABOUT CONTROLLING YOUR EMOTIONS

Feelings can be a little like our laundry. Sometimes we can't sort them out until we dump them out.
BETH MOORE

I do not need to feel good or be ecstatic in order to be in the center of God's will.
BILL BRIGHT

Do the present duty—bear the present pain— enjoy the present pleasure— and leave emotions and "experiences" to look after themselves.
C. S. LEWIS

We need to be able to make decisions based on what we know rather than on what we feel.
JOYCE MEYER

MORE FROM GOD'S WORD

*Grow a wise heart—you'll do yourself a favor;
keep a clear head—you'll find a good life.*
PROVERBS 19:8 MSG

*And let the peace of God rule
in your hearts, to which also you
were called in one body; and be thankful.*
COLOSSIANS 3:15 NKJV

*These things I have spoken to you,
that in Me you may have peace.
In the world you will have tribulation; but be
of good cheer, I have overcome the world.*
JOHN 16:33 NKJV

REMEMBER THIS

Emotions are contagious. When we're around people who are emotionally distraught, we're tempted to become upset, too, *unless* we maintain a safe psychological distance from the emotional outburst. Also, our minds are like gardens. If we tend them with good thoughts, we reap a bountiful harvest. But if we allow them to be overgrown with negative thoughts, we reap a bitter harvest instead.

A TIMELY TIP

Negative thinking breeds more negative thinking, so if you allow negative thoughts to go unchecked, you might find yourself in a very dark place. To protect yourself from a deluge of negativity, you must learn to monitor your thoughts and catch yourself before pessimistic thoughts are allowed to grow, to invade your heart, and to hijack your emotions.

4

UNDERSTANDING DEPRESSION

What the Bible Says

*He heals the brokenhearted
and binds up their wounds.*
PSALM 147:3 HCSB

It has been said, and with good reason, that depression is the common cold of mental illness. Why? Because depression is such a common malady. But make no mistake: depression is a serious condition that, if untreated, can take a terrible toll on individuals and families alike.

The sadness that accompanies any significant loss is an inescapable fact of life. Throughout our lives, all of us must endure the kinds of deep personal losses that leave us struggling to find hope. But in time, we move beyond our grief as the sadness runs its course and gradually abates. Depression, on the other hand, is a physical and emotional condition that is, in almost all cases, treatable with medication and counseling. Depression is not a disease to be taken lightly. Left untreated, it presents real dangers to patients' physical health and to their emotional well-being.

If you find yourself feeling "blue," perhaps it's a logical reaction to the ups and downs of daily life. But if your feelings of sadness have lasted longer than you think they should—or if someone close to you fears that your sadness may have evolved into clinical depression—it's time to seek professional help.

Here are a few simple guidelines to consider as you make

decisions about possible medical treatment:

If you have persistent urges toward self-destructive behavior, or if you feel as though you have lost the will to live, consult a professional counselor or physician immediately.

If someone you trust urges you to seek counseling, schedule a session with a professionally trained counselor to evaluate your condition.

If you experience persistent and prolonged changes in sleep patterns, or if you experience a significant change in weight (either gain or loss), consult your physician.

If you are plagued by consistent, prolonged, severe feelings of hopelessness, consult a physician, a professional counselor, or your pastor.

In the familiar words of John 10:10, Jesus promises, "I have come that they may have life, and that they may have it more abundantly" (NKJV). And in John 15:11, He states, "These things I have spoken to you, that My joy may remain in you, and that your joy may be full" (NKJV). These two passages make it clear: Jesus intends that we experience lives of joyful abundance through Him. Our duty, as grateful believers, is to do everything we can to receive the joy and abundance that can be ours in Christ, and the word "everything" includes appropriate medical treatment when necessary.

MORE THOUGHTS ABOUT DEPRESSION

Feelings of uselessness and hopelessness are not from God, but from the evil one, the devil, who wants to discourage you and thwart your effectiveness for the Lord.

BILL BRIGHT

*I am sure it is never sadness—a proper,
straight, natural response to loss—
that does people harm, but all the other things,
all the resentment, dismay, doubt, and self-pity
with which it is usually complicated.*
C. S. Lewis

MORE FROM GOD'S WORD

*When I sit in darkness,
the Lord will be a light to me.*
Micah 7:8 NKJV

*Weeping may endure for a night,
but joy cometh in the morning.*
Psalm 30:5 KJV

REMEMBER THIS

Depression is serious business, and it's a highly treatable disease. Treat it that way. When you need help, ask for it. Needless suffering is senseless suffering.

A TIMELY TIP

If you're feeling very sad or deeply depressed, talk about it with people who can help. Don't hesitate to speak with your doctor or your pastor or both. Help is available. Ask for it now.

5

GOD WILL HELP YOU MANAGE ANXIETY

What the Bible Says

> *Cast all your anxiety on him because he cares for you.*
> 1 Peter 5:7 NIV

Ours is an anxious generation. We live in an uncertain world—a world where tragedies can befall even the most righteous (and the most innocent) among us. Yet even on those difficult days when our anxieties threaten to overwhelm us, we can be assured that God stands ready to protect us. So, when we are troubled or anxious, we must call upon Him, and in His own time and according to His own plan, He will heal us.

Sometimes our anxieties may stem from physical causes: chemical reactions in the brain that produce severe emotional distress or crippling panic attacks. In such cases, modern medicine offers hope to those who suffer. But oftentimes our anxieties result from spiritual deficits, not physical ones. And when we're spiritually depleted, the best prescription is found not in the medicine cabinet but deep inside the human heart. What we need is a higher daily dose of God's love, God's peace, God's assurance, and God's presence. And how do we acquire these blessings from our Creator? Through prayer, through worship, through fellowship, and through trust.

Prayer is a powerful antidote to anxiety; so, too, is a regular time of devotional reading and meditation. When we spend quiet moments in the divine presence of our heavenly Father, we are reminded once again that our troubles are temporary, but His love is not.

As you face the inevitable challenges of everyday living, do you find yourself becoming anxious, troubled, discouraged, or fearful? If so, turn every one of your concerns over to your heavenly Father. The same God who created the universe will comfort you if you ask Him. Your job, simply put, is to ask Him.

MORE THOUGHTS ABOUT ANXIETY

Anxiety does not empty tomorrow of its sorrows, but only empties today of its strength.
C. H. Spurgeon

Some people feel guilty about their anxieties and regard them as a defect of faith, but they are afflictions, not sins. Like all afflictions, they are, if we can so take them, our share in the passion of Christ.
C. S. Lewis

So often we pray and then fret anxiously, waiting for God to hurry up and do something. All the while God is waiting for us to calm down, so He can do something through us.
Corrie ten Boom

We must lay our questions, frustrations, anxieties, and impotence at the feet of God and wait for His answer. And then receiving it, we must live by faith.
Kay Arthur

*Worry and anxiety are sand
in the machinery of life; faith is the oil.*
E. STANLEY JONES

MORE FROM GOD'S WORD

*Therefore do not worry about tomorrow,
for tomorrow will worry about its own things.
Sufficient for the day is its own trouble.*
MATTHEW 6:34 NKJV

*Peace I leave with you; My peace I give to you;
not as the world gives do I give to you.
Do not let your hearts be troubled, nor fearful.*
JOHN 14:27 NASB

*Let not your heart be troubled;
you believe in God, believe also in Me.*
JOHN 14:1 NKJV

REMEMBER THIS

God always keeps His promises. Remembering His faithfulness in the past can give you peace for today and hope for tomorrow.

A TIMELY TIP

If anxious feelings become debilitating—or if you're unable to sleep because of racing thoughts or irrational worries—consult your physician. Your anxiety may have physical causes that are contributing to your distress. Help is available. Ask for it.

6

A MORNING DEVOTIONAL WILL HELP YOU PREPARE FOR THE DAY AHEAD

What the Bible Says

Morning by morning he wakens me and opens my understanding to his will. The Sovereign Lord has spoken to me, and I have listened.

ISAIAH 50:4–5 NLT

A great way to prepare for the rigors of everyday living is by spending a few moments with God every morning. So if you find that you're simply "too busy" for a daily chat with your heavenly Father, it's time to take a long, hard look at your priorities.

Each day has 1,440 minutes. Do you value your relationship with God enough to spend a few of those minutes with Him? He deserves that much of your time and more. Whether you're dealing with roller-coaster emotions, or stressful circumstances, or any other challenge for that matter, you need God's guidance. So as you consider your plans for the day ahead, here's a tip: organize your life around this simple principle: God first.

When you place your Creator where He belongs—at the very center of your day and your life—you'll accomplish more and worry less because you'll be reminded, yet again, that the Lord is, indeed, your shepherd and that you are protected.

MORE THOUGHTS ABOUT YOUR DAILY DEVOTIONAL

*Begin each day with God.
It will change your priorities.*
Elizabeth George

*Make it the first morning business of your life
to understand some part of the Bible clearly,
and make it your daily business to obey it.*
John Ruskin

*Whatever is your best time in the day,
give that to communion with God.*
Hudson Taylor

*Relying on God has to begin all over again every
day as if nothing had yet been done.*
C. S. Lewis

Doesn't God deserve the best minutes of your day?
Billy Graham

*The amount of time we spend with Jesus—
meditating on His Word and His majesty,
seeking His face—establishes our
fruitfulness in the kingdom.*
Charles Stanley

MORE FROM GOD'S WORD

But grow in the grace and knowledge of our Lord and Savior Jesus Christ. To Him be the glory both now and to the day of eternity.
2 PETER 3:18 HCSB

Heaven and earth will pass away, but My words will never pass away.
MATTHEW 24:35 HCSB

Thy word is a lamp unto my feet, and a light unto my path.
PSALM 119:105 KJV

REMEMBER THIS

A regular time of quiet reflection, prayer, and Bible study will allow you to praise your Creator, to focus your thoughts, and to seek God's guidance on matters great and small.

A TIMELY TIP

Would you like a foolproof formula for a better life? Here it is: stay in close contact with God by scheduling a meeting with Him every morning.

7

MAINTAIN THE RIGHT KIND OF ATTITUDE

What the Bible Says

You must have the same attitude that Christ Jesus had.
PHILIPPIANS 2:5 NLT

Attitudes are the mental filters through which we view and interpret the world around us. Positive attitudes produce positive emotions; negative attitudes don't.

The quality of your attitude will help determine the quality of your life, so you must guard your thoughts accordingly. If you make up your mind to approach life with a healthy mixture of realism and optimism, you'll be rewarded. But if you allow yourself to fall into the unfortunate habit of negative thinking, you may doom yourself to unhappiness or mediocrity or worse.

So the next time you find yourself dwelling upon the negative aspects of your life, refocus your attention on things positive. The next time you find yourself falling prey to the blight of pessimism, stop yourself and turn your thoughts around. The next time you're tempted to waste valuable time gossiping or complaining, resist those temptations. Instead, count your blessings, not your hardships. And thank the Giver of all things good for gifts that are, when you stop to think about it, simply too numerous to count.

MORE THOUGHTS ABOUT ATTITUDE

*The things we think are the things that feed our
souls. If we think on pure and lovely things,
we shall grow pure and lovely like them;
the converse is equally true.*

Hannah Whitall Smith

*We choose what attitudes we have right now.
And it's a continuing choice.*

John Maxwell

*Developing a positive attitude means
working continually to find
what is uplifting and encouraging.*

Barbara Johnson

*Your attitude, not your aptitude,
will determine your altitude.*

Zig Ziglar

*The longer I live, the more convinced I become
that life is 10 percent what happens to us
and 90 percent how we respond to it.*

Charles Swindoll

MORE FROM GOD'S WORD

*This is the day the Lord has made;
let us rejoice and be glad in it.*
PSALM 118:24 HCSB

*A merry heart makes a
cheerful countenance.*
PROVERBS 15:13 NKJV

*Rejoice always;
pray without ceasing.*
1 THESSALONIANS 5:16–17 NASB

REMEMBER THIS

Oftentimes happiness is simply a matter of focusing more intently on God's blessings. So it's important to focus your thoughts on the positive aspects of life, not the negative ones.

A TIMELY TIP

As a Christian, you have every reason on earth—and in heaven—to have a positive attitude. After all, the Lord is in charge. He loves you, and He's prepared a place for you to live eternally with Him. To improve your attitude, focus more intently on God's blessings. When you do, you'll be grateful, not grumpy.

8

TREATING PTSD

What the Bible Says

*Blessed are those who mourn,
for they shall be comforted.*

MATTHEW 5:4 NKJV

Post-traumatic stress disorder (PTSD) is an anxiety disorder that occurs after a highly stressful, deeply disturbing event. People who suffer from PTSD may have insomnia, flashbacks, panic attacks, or low self-esteem. They may also experience emotional numbing, hypervigilance, suicidal thoughts, or a host of other debilitating symptoms. So it's clear that PTSD is a serious psychological and medical condition that should be treated by trained counselors and medical professionals.

Response to trauma is a highly individualized experience: What's traumatic to one person may not be traumatic to another. That being said, there are still certain experiences that make PTSD more likely. People who experience war, assault, a serious accident, or a natural disaster are obviously at risk. Generally speaking, women are at greater risk of PTSD than men.

If you or someone you love has experienced a traumatic event, don't hesitate to ask for help. It's better to seek help and recover than to "tough it out" and suffer.

MORE FROM GOD'S WORD

He Himself is our peace.

EPHESIANS 2:14 NASB

Come unto me, all ye that labor and are heavy laden, and I will give you rest.
MATTHEW 11:28 KJV

And the peace of God, which transcends all understanding, will guard your hearts and your minds in Christ Jesus.
PHILIPPIANS 4:7 NIV

Peace I leave with you, My peace I give to you; not as the world gives do I give to you. Let not your heart be troubled, neither let it be afraid.
JOHN 14:27 NKJV

"I will give peace, real peace, to those far and near, and I will heal them," says the LORD.
ISAIAH 57:19 NCV

REMEMBER THIS

Never lose sight of God's promises. His guidebook, the Holy Bible, contains eternal truths that offer you courage, hope, and emotional health. Trust God's promises.

A TIMELY TIP

Post-traumatic stress disorder (PTSD) is a treatable condition. If you suspect that you or someone you care about may be suffering from PTSD, please seek professional help immediately. PTSD can be treated with medications or psychotherapy or both. Help is available. Ask for it today.

9

EMOTIONS ARE CONTAGIOUS

What the Bible Says

Bad temper is contagious—don't get infected.
Proverbs 22:25 MSG

Emotional highs and lows are contagious. When we're surrounded by people with positive attitudes, we tend to think positively. But when we're surrounded by people whose emotions are negative, we may become infected.

Negative feelings can rob us of the peace and abundance that would otherwise be ours through Christ. So when anger or anxiety separates us from the spiritual blessings that God has in store, we must rethink our priorities. And we must place faith above feelings.

Human emotions are highly variable, decidedly unpredictable, highly contagious, and often unreliable. So we must learn to live by faith, and we must strive, as best we can, to surround ourselves with people who, by their positive attitudes and positive examples, help us understand that all our problems and challenges are temporary, but God's love lasts forever.

MORE FROM GOD'S WORD

Everyone must be quick to hear, slow to speak, and slow to anger, for man's anger does not accomplish God's righteousness.
James 1:19–20 HCSB

> *But stay away from those who have foolish arguments and talk about useless family histories and argue and quarrel about the law. Those things are worth nothing and will not help anyone.*
>
> Titus 3:9 NCV

> *Fools give full vent to their rage,*
> *but the wise bring calm in the end.*
>
> Proverbs 29:11 NIV

> *Stop being angry! Turn from your rage!*
> *Do not lose your temper—*
> *it only leads to harm.*
>
> Psalm 37:8 NLT

> *Do not be conquered by evil,*
> *but conquer evil with good.*
>
> Romans 12:21 HCSB

REMEMBER THIS

Since your emotions will tend to mirror the people around you, it pays to surround yourself with people who make you feel better about yourself, your situation, and your faith.

A TIMELY TIP

The friends you choose can make a profound impact on every aspect of your life, so choose carefully and prayerfully. And while you're choosing, remember that you have every right to select friends who contribute to your spiritual, physical, and emotional health.

10

IMPULSIVITY CAN BE HAZARDOUS TO YOUR EMOTIONAL HEALTH

What the Bible Says

Enthusiasm without knowledge is no good; haste makes mistakes.

PROVERBS 19:2 NLT

Do your emotions sometimes cause you to react impulsively? When you encounter a person with a difficult personality, do you sometimes respond without thinking? Or when you find yourself in a difficult situation, do you react first and think about the consequences of your reaction second? If so, you are certainly not alone. We human beings are emotional by nature, and as a consequence, our emotions sometimes get the better of us.

The Bible teaches us to be self-controlled, thoughtful, and mature, yet the world often tempts us to behave otherwise. Everywhere we turn, or so it seems, we see undisciplined, unruly role models who behave impulsively yet experience few, if any, negative consequences. So it's not surprising that when we find ourselves in stressful situations, we're tempted to respond in undisciplined, unruly ways. But there's a catch: if we fall prey to immaturity or impulsivity, those behaviors inevitably cause many more problems than they solve.

The next time you're tempted to make an impulsive decision, slow down, think things over, and contemplate the consequences of your behavior before you act, not after. When you make a habit of thinking first and acting second, you'll be comforted in the knowledge that you're incorporating God's wisdom into the fabric of your life. And you'll earn the rewards that the Creator inevitably bestows upon people who take the time to look—and to think—before they leap.

MORE THOUGHTS ABOUT IMPULSIVITY

*Nothing is more terrible
than activity without insight.*
THOMAS CARLYLE

*We must learn to wait. There is grace
supplied to the one who waits.*
LETTIE COWMAN

Patience is the companion of wisdom.
ST. AUGUSTINE

Zeal without knowledge is fire without light.
THOMAS FULLER

*In times of uncertainty, wait. Always,
if you have any doubt, wait. Do not force yourself
to any action. If you have a restraint in your spirit,
wait until all is clear, and do not go against it.*
LETTIE COWMAN

He who hesitates is sometimes saved.
JAMES THURBER

MORE FROM GOD'S WORD

*A prudent person foresees
the danger ahead and takes precautions.
The simpleton goes blindly on
and suffers the consequences.*
Proverbs 22:3 NLT

*Do you see a man who speaks too soon?
There is more hope for a fool than for him.*
Proverbs 29:20 HCSB

A patient spirit is better than a proud spirit.
Ecclesiastes 7:8 HCSB

REMEMBER THIS

If you can't seem to put the brakes on impulsive behavior, perhaps you're not praying hard enough. If you tend to think before you act or look before you leap, ask God to help you slow down and make smarter decisions.

A TIMELY TIP

When you find yourself in a frustrating situation, the smartest thing you can do is to take a deep breath, count to ten, say a quick, silent prayer, and collect your thoughts before you act. When you take time to think and pray, you'll probably make smarter choices.

11

CHRONIC NEGATIVITY IS AN EMOTIONAL DEAD END

What the Bible Says

*In my distress I prayed to the Lord,
and the Lord answered me and set me free.*
PSALM 118:5 NLT

From experience, we know that it is easier to criticize than to correct; we understand that it is easier to find faults than to find solutions; and we realize that excessive criticism is usually destructive, not productive. Yet the urge to criticize remains a powerful temptation for most of us.

In the book of James, we are issued a clear warning: "Don't criticize one another, brothers" (4:11 HCSB). Undoubtedly, James understood the paralyzing power of chronic negativity. Negativity is highly contagious: we give it to others who, in turn, give it back to us. Thankfully, this cycle can be broken by positive thoughts, heartfelt prayers, and encouraging words.

As you examine the quality of your own communications, can you honestly say that you're a booster, not a critic, and an optimist, not a pessimist? If so, keep up the good work and the good words. But if you're occasionally overwhelmed by negativity, and if you pass that negativity along to your neighbors, it's time for a mental housecleaning. As a thoughtful Christian, you can use the transforming power of Christ's love to break the chains of negativity. The Lord wants you to be hopeful, helpful, and encouraging. Your intentions should be the same.

MORE THOUGHTS ABOUT AVOIDING NEGATIVITY

Avoid arguments, but when a negative attitude is expressed, counter it with a positive and optimistic opinion.

NORMAN VINCENT PEALE

Developing a positive attitude means working continually to find what is uplifting and encouraging.

BARBARA JOHNSON

God never promises to remove us from our struggles. He does promise, however, to change the way we look at them.

MAX LUCADO

The things we think are the things that feed our souls. If we think on pure and lovely things, we shall grow pure and lovely like them; and the converse is equally true.

HANNAH WHITALL SMITH

We choose what attitudes we have right now. And it's a continuing choice.

JOHN MAXWELL

If you keep on saying things are going to be bad, you have a good chance of becoming a prophet.

ISAAC BASHEVIS SINGER

MORE FROM GOD'S WORD

I say to myself, "The Lord is mine, so I hope in him."
LAMENTATIONS 3:24 NCV

The Lord is good to those who wait for Him, to the soul who seeks Him. It is good that one should hope and wait quietly for the salvation of the Lord.
LAMENTATIONS 3:25–26 NKJV

Hope deferred makes the heart sick.
PROVERBS 13:12 NKJV

REMEMBER THIS

If your inner voice is like a broken record that keeps repeating negative thoughts, you must guard your heart by training yourself to think thoughts that are more rational, more positive, more forgiving, and less destructive.

A TIMELY TIP

Negative thinking breeds more negative thinking, so it's up to you—and only you—to find ways to eliminate negativity, starting today and continuing every day of your life.

12

GOD WILL HELP YOU DEAL WITH CHANGE

What the Bible Says

To every thing there is a season, and a time to every purpose under the heaven.

ECCLESIASTES 3:1 KJV

Every day that we live, we mortals encounter a multitude of changes—some good, some not so good, and some downright discouraging. And on occasion, all of us must endure life-altering personal losses that leave us heartbroken. When we do, our heavenly Father stands ready to comfort us, to guide us, and, in time, to heal us.

Is the world spinning a little too fast for your liking? Are you facing difficult circumstances or unwelcome changes? If so, please remember that God is far bigger than any problem you may face. So instead of worrying about life's inevitable challenges, put your faith in the Lord and in His only begotten Son. After all, "Jesus Christ is the same yesterday, today, and forever" (Hebrews 13:8 NKJV). And it is precisely because Jesus does not change that you can face your own challenges with courage for today and hope for tomorrow.

Are you anxious about situations that you cannot control? Take your anxieties to God. Are you troubled? Take your troubles to Him. Does your little corner of the universe seem to be trembling beneath your feet? Seek protection from the One who cannot be moved. The same God who created the universe will protect you if you ask Him, so ask Him . . . and then serve Him with willing hands and a trusting heart.

MORE THOUGHTS ABOUT CHANGE

*The world changes—circumstances change,
we change—but God's Word never changes.*
WARREN WIERSBE

*Are you on the eve of change?
Embrace it. Accept it. Don't resist it.
Change is not only a part of life,
change is a necessary part of God's strategy.
To use us to change the world,
He alters our assignments.*
MAX LUCADO

*There are two kinds of pain: the pain
of change and the pain of never
changing and remaining the same.*
JOYCE MEYER

*Change always starts in your mind.
The way you think determines the way you feel,
and the way you feel influences the way you act.*
RICK WARREN

*Grace is the voice that calls us to change
and then gives us the power to pull it off.*
MAX LUCADO

*Very often a change of self is needed
more than a change of scene.*
A. C. BENSON

MORE FROM GOD'S WORD

I am the Lord, and I do not change.
MALACHI 3:6 NLT

*But grow in the grace and knowledge
of our Lord and Savior Jesus Christ.
To Him be the glory both now and forever.
Amen.*
2 PETER 3:18 NKJV

*Then He who sat on the throne said,
"Behold, I make all things new."*
REVELATION 21:5 NKJV

REMEMBER THIS

Change is inevitable; growth is not. God will come to your doorstep on countless occasions with opportunities to learn and to grow, and He will knock. Your challenge, of course, is to open the door.

A TIMELY TIP

If a big change is called for, don't be afraid to make it. Sometimes one big leap is better than a thousand baby steps.

13

WITH GOD'S HELP, YOU CAN LEARN TO DEAL WITH DIFFICULT PEOPLE

What the Bible Says

*Bad temper is contagious—
don't get infected.*
PROVERBS 22:25 MSG

Sometimes people can be cruel, discourteous, untruthful, or rude. When other people do things or say things that are hurtful, you may be tempted to strike back with a verbal salvo of your own. But before you say words that can never be unsaid, slow down, say a quiet prayer, and remember this: God corrects other people's behaviors in His own way, and He doesn't need your help (even if you're totally convinced that you're in the right).

So when other people behave cruelly, foolishly, or impulsively—as they will from time to time—don't allow yourself to become caught up in their emotional distress. Instead, speak up for yourself as politely as you can and, if necessary, walk away. Next, forgive everybody as quickly as you can. Then, get on with your life, and leave the rest up to God.

MORE THOUGHTS ABOUT ANGRY PEOPLE

*Give me such love for God and men
as will blot out all hatred and bitterness.*
DIETRICH BONHOEFFER

*We are all fallen creatures
and all very hard to live with.*
C. S. LEWIS

*How often should you forgive
the other person? Only as many times
as you want God to forgive you!*
MARIE T. FREEMAN

*If you are a Christian, you are not a citizen
of this world trying to get to heaven;
you are a citizen of heaven
making your way through this world.*
VANCE HAVNER

*Whatever a person may be like,
we must still love them because we love God.*
JOHN CALVIN

*With God's help, we have what it takes
to meet all upsetting situations
and to react creatively to them.*
NORMAN VINCENT PEALE

MORE FROM GOD'S WORD

*Mockers can get a whole town agitated,
but those who are wise will calm anger.*
PROVERBS 29:8 NLT

*Stay away from a foolish man;
you will gain no knowledge from his speech.*
PROVERBS 14:7 HCSB

Don't make friends with an angry man, and don't be a companion of a hot-tempered man, or you will learn his ways and entangle yourself in a snare.
PROVERBS 22:24–25 HCSB

REMEMBER THIS

If you find yourself in a relationship that's plagued with difficulties, be sure that you're not the one who's being difficult. Before you accuse someone else of being part of the problem, take a careful look at the person you see in the mirror and make sure that you're not the one who is at fault.

A TIMELY TIP

Pick your friends wisely. If you want to maintain a positive attitude, it's important to associate with people who are upbeat, optimistic, and encouraging. Sometimes misguided people may attempt to alleviate their own pain by inflicting pain upon others. If you find yourself on the receiving end of someone else's wrath or chronic negativity, give yourself permission to walk away.

14

GOD WANTS YOU TO LIVE ABUNDANTLY

What the Bible Says

I have come that they may have life, and that they may have it more abundantly.

John 10:10 NKJV

God has a plan for every facet of your life, and His plan includes provisions for your spiritual, physical, and emotional health. But He expects you to do your fair share of the work.

You inhabit a world that is populated by imperfect people who, quite naturally, behave imperfectly. And when they misbehave, as they will from time to time, you may find it all too easy to strike back without thinking, thus making matters even worse. A far better strategy, of course, is to ask for God's guidance. And you can be sure that whenever you ask for the Lord's help, He will give it.

God's Word promises that He will support you in good times and comfort you in hard times. The Creator of the universe will give you the strength to address any problem, the courage to deal effectively with difficult people, and the ability to live abundantly despite the inevitable challenges of everyday life. So the next time you find yourself in an unfortunate situation, remember that spiritual abundance is always available through Christ. And while you're at it, remember that your heavenly Father never leaves you, not even for a moment. He is always available, always ready to listen, always ready to lead and to heal. When you make a habit of talking to Him early and often, He'll guide you and comfort you every day of your life.

MORE THOUGHTS ABOUT ABUNDANCE

Jesus wants Life for us; Life with a capital L.
JOHN ELDREDGE

God loves you and wants you to experience peace and life—abundant and eternal.
BILLY GRAHAM

God is the giver, and we are the receivers. And His richest gifts are bestowed not upon those who do the greatest things, but upon those who accept His abundance and His grace.
HANNAH WHITALL SMITH

Knowing that your future is absolutely assured can free you to live abundantly today.
SARAH YOUNG

The only way you can experience abundant life is to surrender your plans to Him.
CHARLES STANLEY

It is when we give ourselves to be a blessing that we can specially count on the blessing of God.
ANDREW MURRAY

MORE FROM GOD'S WORD

*May Yahweh bless you and protect you;
may Yahweh make His face
shine on you and be gracious to you.*
Numbers 6:24–25 HCSB

*And God is able to make all grace abound
to you, so that always having all
sufficiency in everything, you may have
an abundance for every good deed.*
2 Corinthians 9:8 NASB

*My cup runs over. Surely goodness and mercy
shall follow me all the days of my life;
and I will dwell in the house of the Lord forever.*
Psalm 23:5–6 NKJV

REMEMBER THIS

Jesus came to this earth so that we might experience life abundant and life eternal. Our task, of course, is to obey, to pray, to work, and to accept His abundance with open arms.

A TIMELY TIP

God's blessings are always available. Even when you're dealing with a situation that has unsettled your emotions, the Lord is constantly offering you His abundance and His peace. So remember that you can still find peace amid the storm if you guard your thoughts, if you do your best, and if you leave the rest up to Him.

15

GOD DOESN'T INTEND FOR YOU TO BURN OUT PHYSICALLY OR EMOTIONALLY

What the Bible Says

But those who wait on the Lord shall renew their strength; they shall mount up with wings like eagles, they shall run and not be weary, they shall walk and not faint.

Isaiah 40:31 NKJV

Through His only begotten Son, God offers a peace that passes human understanding, but He won't force His peace upon us; in order to experience it, we must slow down long enough to sense His presence and His love.

Time is a nonrenewable gift from the Lord. How will you use it? You know from experience that you should invest some time each day in yourself, but finding time to do so is easier said than done. As a busy citizen of the twenty-first century, you may have difficulty investing large blocks of time in much-needed thought and self-reflection. If so, it may be time to reorder your priorities.

If you don't prioritize your day, other people will. Before you know it, you'll be taking on lots of new commitments, doing many things, but doing few things well. The Lord, on the other hand, encourages you to slow down, to quiet yourself, and to spend time with Him. And you can be sure that God's way is best.

So how will you organize your life? Will you carve out quiet moments with the Creator? And while you're at it, will you focus your energies and your resources on only the most important tasks on your to-do list? Will you summon the strength to say no when it's appropriate, or will you max out your schedule, leaving much of your most important work undone? Today, slow yourself down, commit more time to the Lord, and spend less time on low-priority tasks. When you do, you'll be amazed at how establishing the right priorities—God's priorities—will revolutionize your life.

MORE THOUGHTS ABOUT STAYING STRONG

There are many burned-out people who think more is always better, who deem it unspiritual to say no.
SARAH YOUNG

Beware of having so much to do that you really do nothing at all because you do not wait upon God to do it aright.
C. H. SPURGEON

The more comfortable we are with mystery in our journey, the more rest we will know along the way.
JOHN ELDREDGE

Every heavy burden you are called upon to lift hides within itself a miraculous secret of strength.
LETTIE COWMAN

God specializes in giving people a fresh start.
RICK WARREN

MORE FROM GOD'S WORD

Careful planning puts you ahead in the long run; hurry and scurry puts you further behind.
PROVERBS 21:5 MSG

Abundant peace belongs to those who love Your instruction; nothing makes them stumble.
PSALM 119:165 HCSB

But godliness with contentment is a great gain.
1 TIMOTHY 6:6 HCSB

REMEMBER THIS

God wants to give you peace, and He wants to repair your frayed emotions. It's up to you to slow down and give Him a chance to do so.

A TIMELY TIP

The Lord can make all things new, including you. When you're emotionally distraught, slow down, say a silent prayer, and focus on God's promises. And while you're at it, remember that the Lord can renew your spirit and restore your strength. Your job, of course, is to let Him.

16

IT'S WISE TO AVOID DEAD-END ARGUMENTS

What the Bible Says

*Avoiding a fight is a mark of honor;
only fools insist on quarreling.*

PROVERBS 20:3 NLT

Time and again, God's Word warns us against angry outbursts and needless arguments. Arguments are seldom won but often lost, so when we acquire the unfortunate habit of continual bickering, we do harm to our friends, to our families, to our coworkers, and to ourselves. So it's no surprise that when we engage in petty squabbles, our losses usually outpace our gains.

If you're dealing with a difficult person, you may be tempted to "take the bait" and argue about matters great and small. If you find yourself in this predicament, take a deep breath, say a silent prayer, and calm yourself down. Arguments are usually a monumental waste of time and energy. And since you're unlikely to win many arguments anyway, there's no rational reason to participate.

Your words have echoes that extend beyond the here and now. So avoid anguished outpourings. Suppress your impulsive outbursts. Curb the need to criticize. Terminate tantrums. Learn to speak words that lift others up as you share a message of encouragement and hope with a world that needs both. And when you talk, choose the very same words that you would use if Jesus were listening to your every word. Because He is.

MORE THOUGHTS ABOUT ARGUMENTS

Argument is the worst sort of conversation.
JONATHAN SWIFT

Most serious conflicts evolve from our attempts to control others who will not accept our control.
WILLIAM GLASSER

An argument seldom convinces anyone contrary to his inclinations.
THOMAS FULLER

Never persist in trying to set people right.
HANNAH WHITALL SMITH

Whatever you do when conflicts arise, be wise. Fight against jumping to quick conclusions and seeing only your side. There are always two sides on the streets of conflict. Look both ways.
CHARLES SWINDOLL

MORE FROM GOD'S WORD

People with quick tempers cause trouble, but those who control their tempers stop a quarrel.
PROVERBS 15:18 NCV

If any man among you seem to be religious, and bridleth not his tongue, but deceiveth his own heart, this man's religion is vain.
JAMES 1:26 KJV

A soft answer turneth away wrath: but grievous words stir up anger.
PROVERBS 15:1 KJV

REMEMBER THIS

Arguments usually cause many more problems than they solve. And if you're dealing with a highly emotional person, you probably won't win the argument anyway. So don't be afraid to leave the scene of an argument rather than engage in a debate that cannot be won.

A TIMELY TIP

If you "win" an argument, what have your really accomplished? Not much. So think twice (or thrice) before you allow yourself to be dragged into a disagreement that's not worth disagreeing about.

17

DRAW CONFIDENCE FROM GOD

What the Bible Says

*Let us hold tightly without wavering
to the hope we affirm,
for God can be trusted to keep his promise.*

Hebrews 10:23 NLT

Are you confident about your future, or do you live under a cloud of uncertainty and doubt? If you trust God's promises, you have every reason to live comfortably and confidently. But despite God's promises and despite His blessings, you may, from time to time, find yourself being tormented by negative emotions. If so, it's time to redirect your thoughts and your prayers.

Even the most optimistic men and women may be overcome by occasional bouts of fear and doubt. You are no different. But even when you feel discouraged—or worse—you should remember that God is always faithful and that you are always protected.

Every life, including yours, is a series of successes and failures, celebrations and disappointments, joys and sorrows, hopes and doubts. But even when you feel very distant from God, remember that He is never distant from you. When you sincerely seek His presence, He will touch your heart, calm your fears, and restore your confidence. No challenge is too big for Him. Not even yours.

MORE THOUGHTS ABOUT CONFIDENCE

One of the marks of spiritual maturity is the quiet confidence that God is in control, without the need to understand why He does what He does.

CHARLES SWINDOLL

When a train goes through a tunnel and it gets dark, you don't throw away your ticket and jump off. You sit still and trust the engineer.

CORRIE TEN BOOM

Never yield to gloomy anticipation. Place your hope and confidence in God. He has no record of failure.

LETTIE COWMAN

Faith and obedience are bound up in the same bundle. He that obeys God, trusts God; and he that trusts God, obeys God.

C. H. SPURGEON

Develop a tremendous faith in God and that will give you a humble yet soundly realistic faith in yourself.

NORMAN VINCENT PEALE

Never be afraid to trust an unknown future to a known God.

CORRIE TEN BOOM

MORE FROM GOD'S WORD

For our gospel came not unto you in word only, but also in power, and in the Holy Ghost, and in much assurance.
1 Thessalonians 1:5 KJV

Let us draw near with a true heart in full assurance of faith, our hearts sprinkled clean from an evil conscience and our bodies washed in pure water.
Hebrews 10:22 HCSB

In quietness and in confidence shall be your strength.
Isaiah 30:15 KJV

REMEMBER THIS

As a Christian, you have every reason to be confident about your life, your future, and your eternal destiny. With God as your partner, you have nothing to fear.

A TIMELY TIP

If negative emotions have caused you to doubt your abilities or your opportunities, it's time for a complete spiritual overhaul. God created you for a purpose, and He has important work specifically for you. So don't let anyone steal your joy, your self-confidence, or your faith in your heavenly Father.

18

WHEN YOU GRIEVE, THE LORD OFFERS COMFORT

What the Bible Says

Weeping may endure for a night, but joy comes in the morning.
Psalm 30:5 KJV

Grief visits all of us who live long and love deeply. When we lose a loved one, or when we experience any other profound loss, darkness overwhelms us for a while, and it seems as if our purpose for living has vanished into thin air. Thankfully, God has other plans.

The Christian faith, as communicated through the words of the Holy Bible, is a healing faith. It offers comfort in times of trouble, courage for our fears, and hope instead of hopelessness. God's Word makes it clear: Absolutely nothing is impossible for Him. So the next time you find yourself overwhelmed by feelings of fear or doubt, refocus your thoughts and redouble your prayers.

Living with intense grief is a marathon, not a sprint. It is a journey that unfolds day by day, and that's exactly how often you should seek direction from your Creator: one day at a time, each day followed by the next, without exception. And please remember that help is always available. First and foremost, you should lean upon the love, help, and support of family members, friends, fellow church members, and your pastor. Other resources include:

- Various local counseling services including, but not limited to, pastoral counselors, psychologists, and community mental health facilities

- Group counseling programs that deal with your specific loss
- Your personal physician
- The local bookstore or library (which will contain specific reading material about your grief and about your particular loss)

If you are experiencing the intense pain of a recent loss, or if you are still mourning a loss from long ago, perhaps you are now ready to begin the next stage of your life. If so, be mindful of this fact: As a wounded survivor, you will have countless opportunities to serve others. And by serving others, you will bring purpose and meaning to the suffering you've endured.

MORE THOUGHTS ABOUT GRIEF

God has enough grace to solve every dilemma you face, wipe every tear you cry, and answer every question you ask.

Max Lucado

If there is something we need more than anything else during grief, it is a friend who stands with us, who doesn't leave us. Jesus is that friend.

Billy Graham

God is sufficient for all our needs, for every problem, for every difficulty, for every broken heart, for every human sorrow.

Peter Marshall

Despair is always the gateway of faith.
OSWALD CHAMBERS

MORE FROM GOD'S WORD

The LORD shall give thee rest from thy sorrow, and from thy fear.
ISAIAH 14:3 KJV

The LORD is near to those who have a broken heart.
PSALM 34:18 NKJV

Ye shall be sorrowful, but your sorrow shall be turned into joy.
JOHN 16:20 KJV

REMEMBER THIS

Of this you can be sure: God's faithfulness is unwavering, and eternal. Because He is faithful, you can—and should—live courageously. And when you're hurting, please remember that your pain is temporary but His love endures forever.

A TIMELY TIP

Grief is not meant to be avoided or feared; it is meant to be worked through. Grief hurts, but denying your true feelings can hurt even more. So don't hesitate to talk about your sorrow with people you trust. And while you're at it, remember this: with God's help, you can face your pain *and* move beyond it.

19

FAILURE ISN'T FINAL

What the Bible Says

For though the righteous fall seven times, they rise again.
PROVERBS 24:16 NIV

If you want to be happy, consistently happy, you must learn how to deal with failure. Why? Because all of us face setbacks from time to time. Our disappointments are simply the price that we must occasionally pay for our willingness to take risks as we follow our dreams. But even when we encounter bitter disappointments, we must never lose faith.

Hebrews 10:36 advises, "Patient endurance is what you need now, so you will continue to do God's will. Then you will receive all that he has promised" (NLT). These words remind us that when we persevere, we will eventually receive the rewards that God has promised us. What's required is perseverance, not perfection.

When we face hardships, the Lord stands ready to protect us. Our responsibility, of course, is to ask Him for protection. When we call upon Him in heartfelt prayer, He will answer—in His own time and according to His own plan—and He will do His part to heal us. And while we are waiting for God's plans to unfold and for His healing touch to restore us, we can be comforted in the knowledge that our Creator can overcome any obstacle, even if we cannot.

MORE THOUGHTS ABOUT OVERCOMING FAILURE

No amount of falls will really undo us if we keep picking ourselves up after each one.
C. S. Lewis

No matter how badly we have failed, we can always get up and begin again. Our God is the God of new beginnings.
Warren Wiersbe

Mistakes offer the possibility for redemption and a new start in God's kingdom. No matter what you're guilty of, God can restore your innocence.
Barbara Johnson

Failure is one of life's most powerful teachers. How we handle our failures determines whether we're going to simply "get by" in life or "press on."
Beth Moore

You may encounter many defeats, but you must not be defeated. In fact, it may be necessary to encounter the defeats, so you can know who you are, what you can rise from, and how you can still come out of it.
Maya Angelou

Those who have failed miserably are often the first to see God's formula for success.
ERWIN LUTZER

MORE FROM GOD'S WORD

Weeping may endure for a night, but joy comes in the morning.
PSALM 30:5 KJV

If you listen to correction to improve your life, you will live among the wise.
PROVERBS 15:31 NCV

But as for you, be strong; don't be discouraged, for your work has a reward.
2 CHRONICLES 15:7 HCSB

REMEMBER THIS

Setbacks are inevitable, but your response to them is optional. You and the Lord, working together, can always find a way to turn a stumbling block into a stepping stone, so don't give up hope. Better days will arrive, and perhaps sooner than you think.

A TIMELY TIP

When you're discouraged, disappointed, or hurt, don't spend too much time asking, "Why me, Lord?" Instead, ask, "What now, Lord?" and then get busy. When you do, you'll feel much better.

20

BEWARE OF BITTERNESS

What the Bible Says

Let all bitterness, wrath, anger, clamor, and evil speaking be put away from you, with all malice. And be kind to one another, tenderhearted, forgiving one another, just as God in Christ forgave you.
EPHESIANS 4:31–32 NKJV

Bitterness is a spiritual sickness. It will consume your soul; it is dangerous to your emotional health; it can destroy you if you let it. The world holds few if any rewards for those who remain angrily focused upon the past. Still, the act of forgiveness is difficult for all but the most saintly men and women. Being frail, fallible, imperfect human beings, most of us are quick to anger, quick to blame, slow to forgive, and even slower to forget.

If you are caught up in intense feelings of anger or resentment, you know all too well the destructive power of these emotions. How can you rid yourself of these feelings? First, you must prayerfully ask God to cleanse your heart. Then, you must learn to catch yourself whenever angry thoughts begin to invade your consciousness. You must learn to resist those negative thoughts before they hijack your emotions.

When you learn to direct your thoughts toward more positive topics, you'll be protected from the spiritual and emotional consequences of bitterness. And you'll be wiser, healthier, and happier too.

MORE THOUGHTS ABOUT THE DANGER OF BITTERNESS

Bitterness imprisons life; love releases it.
HARRY EMERSON FOSDICK

Bitterness sentences you to relive the hurt over and over.
LEE STROBEL

Bitterness is anger gone sour, an attitude of deep discontent that poisons our souls and destroys our peace.
BILLY GRAHAM

Bitterness is a spiritual cancer, a rapidly growing malignancy that can consume your life. Bitterness cannot be ignored but must be healed at the very core, and only Christ can heal bitterness.
BETH MOORE

Resentment or grudges do no harm to the person against whom you hold these feelings, but every day and every night of your life, they are eating at you.
NORMAN VINCENT PEALE

Life is certainly too brief to waste even a single moment on animosity.
CARDINAL JOSEPH BERNADINE

MORE FROM GOD'S WORD

Do not judge, and you will not be judged.
Do not condemn, and you will not be condemned.
Forgive, and you will be forgiven.
Luke 6:37 HCSB

Do not repay anyone evil for evil.
Try to do what is honorable in everyone's eyes.
Romans 12:17 HCSB

The heart knows its own bitterness,
and a stranger does not share its joy.
Proverbs 14:10 NKJV

REMEMBER THIS

You can never fully enjoy the present if you're bitter about the past. So instead of living in the past, make peace with it . . . and move on.

A TIMELY TIP

The Bible warns that bitterness is both dangerous and self-destructive. So today, make a list of the people you need to forgive and the things you need to forget. Then ask God to give you the strength to forgive and move on.

21

YOU CAN LEARN TO CONTROL ANGER BEFORE IT CONTROLS YOU

What the Bible Says

Everyone must be quick to hear, slow to speak, and slow to anger, for man's anger does not accomplish God's righteousness.
James 1:19–20 HCSB

Anger is a natural human emotion that is sometimes necessary and appropriate. Even Jesus became angry when confronted with the money changers in the temple:

> And Jesus entered the temple and drove out all those who were buying and selling in the temple, and overturned the tables of the money changers and the seats of those who were selling doves (Matthew 21:12 NASB).

Righteous indignation is an appropriate response to evil, but God does not intend that anger should rule our lives. Far from it. The Lord intends that we turn away from anger whenever possible and forgive our neighbors just as we seek forgiveness for ourselves.

Life is full of frustrations: some great and some small. On occasion, you, like Jesus, will confront evil, and when you do, you may respond as He did: vigorously and without reservation. But more often, your frustrations will be of the more mundane variety. As long as you live here on earth, you will face countless opportunities to lose your temper over small, relatively insignificant events: a traffic jam, a spilled cup of coffee, an inconsiderate comment, or a broken promise. When you are tempted to lose your temper over the minor inconveniences of life, don't. Turn away from anger, hatred, bitterness, and regret. Turn instead to God. When you do, you'll be following His commandments and giving yourself a priceless gift: the gift of peace.

MORE THOUGHTS ABOUT ANGER

*Anger and bitterness—whatever the cause—
only end up hurting us. Turn that anger over to Christ.*
BILLY GRAHAM

*Frustration is not the will of God.
There is time to do anything
and everything that God wants us to do.*
ELISABETH ELLIOT

*Every stroke our fury strikes is sure
to hit ourselves at last.*
WILLIAM PENN

*Hence it is not enough to deal with the temper.
We must go to the source, and change
the inmost nature, and the angry feelings
will die away of themselves.*
HENRY DRUMMOND

Hot heads and cold hearts never solved anything.
BILLY GRAHAM

MORE FROM GOD'S WORD

Do not let the sun go down on your anger, and do not give the devil an opportunity.
EPHESIANS 4:26–27 NASB

He who is slow to wrath has great understanding, but he who is impulsive exalts folly.
PROVERBS 14:29 NKJV

But now you must also put away all the following: anger, wrath, malice, slander, and filthy language from your mouth.
COLOSSIANS 3:8 HCSB

REMEMBER THIS

Angry outbursts can be dangerous to your emotional and spiritual health, not to mention your relationships. So treat anger as an uninvited guest, and usher it away as quickly—and as quietly—as possible.

A TIMELY TIP

Don't allow yourself to be caught up in another person's emotional outbursts. Emotions are highly contagious, and angry encounters almost never have happy endings. So if someone is ranting, raving, or worse, you have the right to leave the scene of the argument.

22

NAVIGATING DIFFICULT RELATIONSHIPS

What the Bible Says

It is safer to meet a bear robbed of her cubs than to confront a fool caught in foolishness.
Proverbs 17:12 NLT

Emotional health is contagious, and so is emotional distress. If you're fortunate enough to be surrounded by family members and friends who celebrate life and praise God, consider yourself profoundly blessed. But if you find yourself caught in an unhealthy, discouraging relationship, it's time to look realistically at your situation, and it's probably time to begin making some changes.

Don't worry about changing other people; you can't do it. What you can do is to conduct yourself in a responsible fashion and insist that other people treat you with the dignity and consideration that you deserve.

Don't be discouraged. God has grand plans for your life, and He has promised that joy and abundance that can be yours through Him. But to fully experience God's gifts, you need happy, emotionally healthy people to share them with. It's up to you to make sure that you do your part to build the kinds of relationships that will bring abundance to you, to your family, and to God's world.

MORE THOUGHTS ABOUT DEALING WITH DISCOURAGEMENT

*Just as courage is faith in good,
so discouragement is faith in evil, and,
while courage opens the door to good,
discouragement opens it to evil.*

Hannah Whitall Smith

*Discouraged people don't need critics.
They hurt enough already. What they need
is encouragement. They need a refuge,
a willing, caring, available someone.*

Charles Swindoll

*Feelings of uselessness and hopelessness
are not from God, but from the evil one,
the devil, who wants to discourage you
and thwart your effectiveness for the Lord.*

Bill Bright

*The biggest disease today is not leprosy
or tuberculosis, but rather the feeling
of being unwanted.*

Mother Teresa

*If I am asked how we are to get rid
of discouragements, I can only say,
as I have had to say of so many other wrong
spiritual habits, we must give them up.*

Hannah Whitall Smith

*If your hopes are being disappointed just now,
it means that they are being purified.*

OSWALD CHAMBERS

MORE FROM GOD'S WORD

If God is for us, who is against us?
ROMANS 8:31 HCSB

The Lord is a refuge for His people and a stronghold.
JOEL 3:16 NASB

God shall wipe away all tears from their eyes.
REVELATION 7:17 KJV

REMEMBER THIS

Unless the person you're trying to change is a young child, and unless and you are that child's parent or guardian, don't try to change him or her. Why? Because people change when they want to, not when you want them to.

A TIMELY TIP

If you're caught in a troubled relationship, don't be discouraged and don't give up hope. There's always something you can do to make your life better, even if it means breaking off the relationship. Tough times never last, but determined, optimistic, faith-filled people—people like you—do.

23

WHEN YOUR HEART IS TROUBLED, HAVE COURAGE

What the Bible Says

For God has not given us a spirit of fearfulness, but one of power, love, and sound judgment.

2 Timothy 1:7 HCSB

Every person's life is a tapestry of events: some wonderful, some not so wonderful, and some downright disastrous. When we visit the mountaintops of life, praising God isn't hard—in fact, it's easy. In our moments of triumph, we can bow our heads and thank the Lord for our victories. But when we fail to reach the mountaintops, when we endure the inevitable losses that are a part of every person's life, we find it much tougher to give God the praise He deserves. Yet wherever we find ourselves, whether on the mountaintops or in the darkest valleys, we must still offer thanks to our Creator, giving thanks in all circumstances.

God is not a distant being. He is not absent from our world, nor is He absent from your world. The Lord is not "out there"; He is "right here," continuously reshaping His universe, and continuously reshaping the lives of those who dwell in it.

Your heavenly Father is with you always, listening to your thoughts and prayers, watching over your every move. If the demands of everyday life weigh down upon you, you may be tempted to ignore His presence or—worse yet—to lose faith in His promises. But when you quiet yourself and acknowledge His presence, God will touch your heart and restore your courage. And because your Creator cares for you and protects you, you can rise above your fears.

MORE THOUGHTS ABOUT COURAGE

In my experience, God rarely makes our fear disappear. Instead, He asks us to be strong and take courage.
BRUCE WILKINSON

Courage is not simply one of the virtues, but the form of every virtue at the testing point.
C. S. LEWIS

Take courage. We walk in the wilderness today and in the Promised Land tomorrow.
D. L. MOODY

God's power is great enough for our deepest desperation. You can go on. You can pick up the pieces and start anew. You can face your fears. You can find peace in the rubble. There is healing for your soul.
SUZANNE DALE EZELL

When we face our fears, we can find our freedom.
JOYCE MEYER

Do not limit the limitless God! With Him, face the future unafraid because you are never alone.
LETTIE COWMAN

MORE FROM GOD'S WORD

*Behold, God is my salvation;
I will trust, and not be afraid.*
Isaiah 12:2 KJV

*Be on guard. Stand firm in the faith.
Be courageous. Be strong.*
1 Corinthians 16:13 NLT

*But He said to them,
"It is I; do not be afraid."*
John 6:20 NKJV

REMEMBER THIS

You and God, working together, can handle absolutely anything that comes your way. So hold fast to God's promises and pray. The Lord will give you the strength to meet any challenge if you ask Him sincerely and often.

A TIMELY TIP

It takes insight and courage to deal effectively with negative emotions. If you need insight, talk to people you trust and spend time studying God's Word. And if you need courage, ask the Lord to help you do what needs to be done.

24

GUARD YOUR HEART

What the Bible Says

*Guard your heart above all else,
for it is the source of life.*
Proverbs 4:23 HCSB

When our emotions get the best of us, we are tempted to respond in vindictive, aggressive ways. Yet God's Word is clear: We are to guard our hearts "above all else." So how should we respond to the difficult people and troubling circumstances that complicate our lives and rouse our emotions? We must react fairly, honestly, and maturely, and we must never betray our Christian values.

Here in the twenty-first century, distractions, frustrations, and angry eruptions are woven into the fabric of everyday life. Many famous people seem to take pride in discourteous behavior, and social media has dramatically increased our contact with troubled personalities. As believers, we must remain vigilant. Not only must we resist Satan when he confronts us, but we must also avoid the people and the places where Satan can most easily tempt or confuse us.

Do you seek God's peace and His blessings? Then guard your heart. When you're tempted to lash out in anger, hold your tongue. When you're faced with a difficult choice or a powerful temptation, seek the Lord's counsel and trust the counsel He gives. When you're uncertain of your next step, take a deep breath, calm yourself, and follow in the footsteps of God's only begotten Son. Invite God into your heart and live according to His commandments. When you do, you will be blessed today, and tomorrow, and forever.

MORE THOUGHTS ABOUT GUARDING YOUR HEART

We have two natures is within us, both struggling for mastery. Which one will dominate us? It depends on which one we feed.

BILLY GRAHAM

There is no neutral ground in the universe: every square inch, every split second, is claimed by God and counterclaimed by Satan.

C. S. LEWIS

Our fight is not against any physical enemy; it is against organizations and powers that are spiritual. We must struggle against sin all our lives, but we are assured we will win.

CORRIE TEN BOOM

The insight that relates to God comes from purity of heart, not from clearness of intellect.

OSWALD CHAMBERS

Our battles are first won or lost in the secret of our will in God's presence, never in full view of the world.

OSWALD CHAMBERS

God is voting for us all the time. The devil is voting against us all the time. The way we vote carries the election.

CORRIE TEN BOOM

MORE FROM GOD'S WORD

Finally, brothers and sisters, whatever is true, whatever is noble, whatever is right, whatever is pure, whatever is lovely, whatever is admirable—if anything is excellent or praiseworthy—think about such things.
PHILIPPIANS 4:8 NIV

Flee from youthful passions, and pursue righteousness, faith, love, and peace, along with those who call on the Lord from a pure heart.
2 TIMOTHY 2:22 HCSB

The one who keeps God's commands lives in him, and he in them. And this is how we know that he lives in us: We know it by the Spirit he gave us.
1 JOHN 3:24 NIV

REMEMBER THIS

If you really want to follow Jesus, you must walk as He walked, and you must strive to lead a righteous life, despite your imperfections. When you strive to please God with your thoughts, prayers, and deeds, you'll be eternally rewarded.

A TIMELY TIP

The Lord wants you to guard your heart from situations or harmful emotions that would drive you away from Him. He wants the best for you, and you should want the same for yourself. How do you achieve the best life has to offer? You must start by guarding your heart.

25

DON'T PANIC!

What the Bible Says

*So we can say with confidence,
"The LORD is my helper, so I will have no fear.
What can mere people do to me?"*
HEBREWS 13:6 NLT

If you've ever experienced a full-blown panic attack, you can attest to the fact that it is a terrifying experience. Your heart beats faster; you can't catch your breath; your emotions are screaming; and you feel frightened beyond words, but your mind tells you there's nothing to be afraid of. To make matters worse, after you've experienced your first attack, you may develop an ongoing fear of having another one.

Panic attacks occur when we experience an exaggerated physical response to a situation that shouldn't be so threatening. Researchers aren't completely clear what causes panic attacks, but they can confirm that these are physiological events that include dramatic increases in both heart rate and adrenaline levels. Fortunately, these attacks are highly treatable with counseling or medication or both.

So if you've found yourself paralyzed by fear without good reason, don't suffer in silence. Instead, speak with your physician and develop a recovery plan. God wants you to experience His joyful abundance, but untreated panic disorders will inevitably get in the way. So don't be afraid or embarrassed to ask for help. It's the surest way to say no to panic and yes to peace.

MORE THOUGHTS ABOUT KNOWING YOU ARE PROTECTED

Are you weak? Weary? Confused? Troubled? Pressured? How is your relationship with God? Is it held in its place of priority? I believe the greater the pressure, the greater your need for time alone with Him.

KAY ARTHUR

Every misfortune, every failure, every loss may be transformed. God has the power to transform all misfortunes into "God-sends."

LETTIE COWMAN

The fierce grip of panic need not immobilize you. God knows no limitation when it comes to deliverance. Admit your fear. Commit it to Him. Dump the pressure on Him. He can handle it.

CHARLES SWINDOLL

Even in the winter, even in the midst of the storm, the sun is still there. Somewhere, up above the clouds, it still shines and warms and pulls at the life buried deep inside the brown branches and frozen earth. The sun is there! Spring will come.

GLORIA GAITHER

As you walk through the valley of the unknown, you will find the footprints of Jesus both in front of you and beside you.

CHARLES STANLEY

MORE FROM GOD'S WORD

Peace I leave with you; My peace I give to you; not as the world gives do I give to you. Do not let your heart be troubled, nor let it be fearful.
JOHN 14:27 NASB

But He said to them, "It is I; do not be afraid."
JOHN 6:20 NKJV

Fear not, for I am with you; be not dismayed, for I am your God. I will strengthen you, yes, I will help you, I will uphold you with My righteous right hand.
ISAIAH 41:10 NKJV

REMEMBER THIS

If you're facing a crisis, don't face it alone. Enlist God's help. And then, when you've finished praying about your problem, don't be afraid to seek help from family, from friends, from a trusted counselor, or from your pastor.

A TIMELY TIP

If you experience a full-blown panic attack, don't try to handle it on your own. Instead, talk to your physician. Medical professionals and knowledgeable counselors can offer solutions, but they won't offer them unless they're asked.

26

YOU CAN FREE YOURSELF FROM THE PAIN OF PERFECTIONISM

What the Bible Says

Those who wait for perfect weather will never plant seeds; those who look at every cloud will never harvest crops. . . . Plant early in the morning, and work until evening, because you don't know if this or that will succeed. They might both do well.

ECCLESIASTES 11:4, 6 NCV

As a citizen of the twenty-first century, you know that demands can be high, and expectations even higher. Traditional media outlets, along with their social-media counterparts, deliver an endless stream of messages that tell you how to look, how to behave, how to eat, and how to dress. And that's only the beginning. If you're not careful, you'll find yourself scrambling to keep up with everybody's expectations, which is impossible.

The world's expectations are impossible to meet—God's are not. The Lord doesn't expect you to be perfect, and neither, by the way, should you.

Remember: The expectations that really matter are God's expectations. Everything else takes a back seat. So do your best to please God, and don't worry too much about what other people think. And when it comes to meeting the unrealistic expectations of a world gone haywire, forget about trying to be perfect—it's impossible.

MORE THOUGHTS ABOUT THE DANGERS OF PERFECTIONISM

The happiest people in the world are not those who have no problems, but the people who have learned to live with those things that are less than perfect.

JAMES DOBSON

The greatest destroyer of good works is the desire to do great works.

C. H. SPURGEON

God is so inconceivably good. He's not looking for perfection. He already saw it in Christ. He's looking for affection.

BETH MOORE

We shall never come to the perfect man till we come to the perfect world.

MATTHEW HENRY

What makes a Christian a Christian is not perfection but forgiveness.

MAX LUCADO

Better to do something imperfectly than to do nothing perfectly.

ROBERT SCHULLER

MORE FROM GOD'S WORD

*Let not your heart be troubled;
you believe in God, believe also in Me.*
JOHN 14:1 NKJV

*In thee, O LORD, do I put my trust:
let me never be put to confusion.*
PSALM 71:1 KJV

*The fear of human opinion disables;
trusting in GOD protects you from that.*
PROVERBS 29:25 MSG

REMEMBER THIS

Don't worry about achieving perfection in this lifetime—it cannot be done. God doesn't want your perfection; He wants your heart. There will be plenty of time for perfection in the world to come.

A TIMELY TIP

In heaven, we will know perfection. Here on earth, we have a few short years to wrestle with the challenges of imperfection. God is perfect; we human beings are not. May we live—and forgive—accordingly.

27

BEYOND SHAME

What the Bible Says

Let us come near to God with a sincere heart and a sure faith, because we have been made free from a guilty conscience, and our bodies have been washed with pure water.

HEBREWS 10:22 NCV

Have you done things you're ashamed of? If so, welcome to a very large club. Even some of the very best people on the planet have done things that only God can forgive. But the good news is this: Whenever we admit our shortcomings to the Lord and ask for His forgiveness, He gives it. There's nothing any of us can do to redeem ourselves from sin; that's something only the Lord can do. So what can we do? We can allow God's Son into our hearts and allow Him to do what we cannot.

Shame is a form of spiritual cancer; it can be deadly, but it is treatable. The treatment begins when we acknowledge our shortcomings and ask for God's mercy. But it doesn't end there. Once God forgives us, we still have work to do: we must forgive ourselves.

The Lord knows all your imperfections, all your faults, and all your mistakes . . . and He loves you anyway. And because God loves you, you can—and should—feel good about the person you see when you look into the mirror.

God's love is bigger and more powerful than anybody (including you) can imagine, but His love is very real. So do yourself a favor right now: Accept God's love with open arms. And while you're at it, remember this: Even when you don't love yourself very much, God loves you. And God is always right.

MORE THOUGHTS ABOUT GUILT AND SHAME

The purpose of guilt is to bring us to Jesus. Once we are there, then its purpose is finished. If we continue to make ourselves guilty— to blame ourselves—then that is a sin in itself.

CORRIE TEN BOOM

The most marvelous ingredient in the forgiveness of God is that He also forgets, the one thing a human being cannot do. With God, forgetting is a divine attribute. God's forgiveness forgets.

OSWALD CHAMBERS

The redemption, accomplished for us by our Lord Jesus Christ on the cross at Calvary, is redemption from the power of sin as well as from its guilt. Christ is able to save all who come unto God by Him.

HANNAH WHITALL SMITH

Guilt is an appalling waste of energy; you can't build on it. It's only good for wallowing in.

KATHERINE MANSFIELD

God does not wish us to remember what He is willing to forget.

GEORGE A. BUTTRICK

MORE FROM GOD'S WORD

Be gracious to me, God, according to Your faithful love; according to Your abundant compassion, blot out my rebellion. Wash away my guilt, and cleanse me from my sin.

Psalm 51:1–2 HCSB

How can I know all the sins lurking in my heart? Cleanse me from these hidden faults. Keep your servant from deliberate sins! Don't let them control me. Then I will be free of guilt and innocent of great sin.

Psalm 19:12–13 NLT

Create in me a pure heart, God, and make my spirit right again.

Psalm 51:10 NCV

REMEMBER THIS

You cannot do anything that God can't forgive, and He forgives you when you ask. The Lord stands ready to forgive. The next move is yours.

A TIMELY TIP

If you've been victimized by shame, it's time to have a heart-to-heart talk with your Creator. If you've asked for the Lord's forgiveness, He has already given it. And because He has forgiven you, you should be quick to forgive yourself and make peace with your past. To do otherwise is to hold yourself to a different standard than God does.

28

TO MAINTAIN EMOTIONAL STABILITY, IT OFTEN HELPS TO ESTABLISH BOUNDARIES

What the Bible Says

Stay away from a fool, for you will not find knowledge on their lips.

PROVERBS 14:7 NIV

In a perfect world filled with perfect people, our relationships, too, would be perfect. But none of us are perfect and neither are our relationships. As we work to make our imperfect relationships a little happier and healthier, we grow as individuals and as families. But if we find ourselves in relationships that are debilitating or dangerous, then changes must be made and appropriate boundaries must be established.

Life is too short to allow another person's problematic personality to invade your psyche and ruin your day. But because human emotions are contagious, there's always the danger that you'll be drawn into the other person's mental state, with predictably negative consequences. A far better strategy is to step back from the situation, to say a silent prayer, and to ask God to help you retain a sense of calm. When you do, He'll answer your prayer, the storm will pass, and you'll be glad you retained your emotional stability, even though some of the people around you were losing theirs.

If you find yourself caught up in a personal relationship that is bringing havoc into your life, and if you can't seem to find the courage to do something about it, don't hesitate to consult your pastor.

Or you may seek the advice of a trusted friend or a professionally trained counselor. But whatever you do, don't be satisfied with the status quo and don't be afraid to establish sensible boundaries that will allow you to maintain your emotional and spiritual health.

MORE THOUGHTS ABOUT PROTECTING YOURSELF

You are justified in avoiding people who send you from their presence with less hope and strength to cope with life's problems than when you met them.
ELLA WHEELER WILCOX

Stay away from fatty foods, hard liquor, and negative people.
MARIE T. FREEMAN

Not everybody is healthy enough to have a front-row seat in your life.
SUSAN L. TAYLOR

It is far better to be alone than to be in bad company.
GEORGE WASHINGTON

No one can drive us crazy unless we give them the keys.
DOUG HORTON

Keep away from people who try to belittle your ambitions.
MARK TWAIN

MORE FROM GOD'S WORD

Be sober, be vigilant; because your adversary the devil walks about like a roaring lion, seeking whom he may devour.
1 Peter 5:8 NKJV

It is better to meet a bear robbed of her cubs than to meet a fool doing foolish things.
Proverbs 17:12 NCV

Do not be deceived: "Bad company corrupts good morals."
1 Corinthians 15:33 HCSB

REMEMBER THIS

If you're a little too anxious to please other people and a little hesitant to set boundaries, God wants to have a little chat with you. Time and again, the Bible teaches us that we can't please all of the people all of the time, nor should we attempt to.

A TIMELY TIP

You can't change other people, but you can change the way that you react to them. If someone is threatening you, either physically or emotionally, you have the right to set boundaries and enforce those boundaries, even if it means separating yourself from that person.

29

YOU CAN TAKE YOUR WORRIES TO GOD AND LEAVE THEM THERE

What the Bible Says

Therefore do not worry about tomorrow, for tomorrow will worry about its own things. Sufficient for the day is its own trouble.

Matthew 6:34 NKJV

Because we are fallible human beings struggling through the inevitable challenges of life here on earth, we worry. Even though we, as Christians, have been promised the gift of eternal life—even though we are blessed by God's love and protection—we find ourselves fretting over the inevitable frustrations of everyday life.

Where is the best place to take your worries? Take them to the Lord. Take your concerns to Him; take your fears to Him; take your doubts to Him; take your weaknesses to Him; take your sorrows to Him . . . and leave them all there. Seek protection from the Creator and build your spiritual house upon the Rock that cannot be moved. Remind yourself that God still sits in His heaven and you are His beloved child. Then, perhaps, you will worry less and trust Him more. And that's as it should be because the Lord is trustworthy . . . and you are protected.

MORE THOUGHTS ABOUT WORRY

Pray, and let God worry.

Martin Luther

Worry is like a rocking chair. It keeps you moving but doesn't get you anywhere.
CORRIE TEN BOOM

MORE FROM GOD'S WORD

Cast your burden on the LORD, and He shall sustain you; He shall never permit the righteous to be moved.
PSALM 55:22 NKJV

Let not your heart be troubled; you believe in God, believe also in Me.
JOHN 14:1 NKJV

Do not be anxious about anything, but in every situation, by prayer and petition, with thanksgiving, present your requests to God.
PHILIPPIANS 4:6 NIV

REMEMBER THIS

God is in control of His world and your world. He understands His plans, even if you do not. Trust Him.

A TIMELY TIP

Divide your areas of concern into two categories: the things you can control and the things you can't. Focus on the former and refuse to waste time or energy worrying about the latter. You have worries, but God has solutions. Your challenge is to trust Him to solve the problems that are simply too big for you to resolve on your own.

30

BEYOND PROCRASTINATION

What the Bible Says

*But prove yourselves doers of the word,
and not merely hearers who delude themselves.*

JAMES 1:22 NASB

If you find yourself bound by the chains of procrastination, ask yourself what you're waiting for—or more accurately what you're afraid of—and why. As you examine the emotional roadblocks that have heretofore blocked your path, you may discover that you're waiting for the "perfect" moment, that instant in time when you feel neither afraid nor anxious. But in truth, perfect moments like those are few and far between. So stop waiting for the perfect moment and focus instead on finding the right moment to do what needs to be done. Then trust God and get busy. When you do, you'll discover that you and the Father, working together, can accomplish great things.

Once you acquire the habit of doing what needs to be done when it needs to be done, you will avoid untold trouble, worry, and stress. So learn to overcome procrastination by paying less attention to your fears and more attention to your responsibilities. God has created a world that punishes procrastinators and rewards people who "do it now." In other words, life doesn't procrastinate. Neither should you.

MORE THOUGHTS ABOUT DEFEATING PROCRASTINATION

Character is formed by doing the thing we are supposed to do, when it should be done, whether we feel like doing it or not.

FATHER FLANAGAN

*Do noble things,
not dream them all day long;
and so make life, death,
and that vast forever one grand, sweet song.*

CHARLES KINGSLEY

*Our grand business is,
not to see what lies dimly at a distance,
but to do what lies closely at hand.*

THOMAS CARLYLE

*Don't wait to "feel" like doing a thing to do it.
Live by decision, not emotion.*

JOYCE MEYER

Every duty which we omit obscures some truth which we should have known.

JOHN RUSKIN

One today is worth two tomorrows.

BEN FRANKLIN

MORE FROM GOD'S WORD

For the kingdom of God is not in talk but in power.
1 CORINTHIANS 4:20 HCSB

Therefore, get your minds ready for action, be serious and set your hope completely on the grace to be brought to you at the revelation of Jesus Christ.
1 PETER 1:13 HCSB

When you make a vow to God, do not delay to fulfill it. He has no pleasure in fools; fulfill your vow.
ECCLESIASTES 5:4 NIV

REMEMBER THIS

Procrastination increases emotions like stress and anxiety; intelligent action decreases these kinds of emotions. It's up to each of us to act accordingly.

A TIMELY TIP

The habit of procrastination is often rooted in the fear of failure, the fear of discomfort, or the fear of embarrassment. Your challenge is to confront these fears and defeat them. So if unpleasant work needs to be done, do it sooner rather than later. It's easy to put off unpleasant tasks, but a far better strategy is this: Do the unpleasant work first so you can enjoy the rest of the day. The sooner you face your problems—and the sooner you begin working to resolve them—the better your life will be.

31

DON'T PLAY THE BLAME GAME

What the Bible Says

*But each person should examine his own work,
and then he will have a reason
for boasting in himself alone,
and not in respect to someone else.
For each person will have to carry his own load.*

Galatians 6:4–5 HCSB

To blame others for our own problems is the height of futility, yet casting blame upon others is a favorite human pastime. Why? Because blaming is much easier than fixing, and because criticizing others is so much easier than improving ourselves. So instead of solving our problems legitimately (by doing the work required to solve them) we are inclined to pass the buck while doing precious little else. When we do, our problems, quite predictably, remain unsolved.

Have you acquired the bad habit of blaming others for problems that you could or should solve yourself? If so, you are wasting time and energy. So instead of looking for someone to blame, look for something to fix, and then get busy fixing it. And as you consider your own situation, remember this: God has a way of helping those who help themselves, but He doesn't spend much time helping those who don't.

MORE THOUGHTS ABOUT BLAMING OTHERS

*Do not think of the faults
of others but what is good
in them and faulty in yourself.*
ST. TERESA OF AVILA

*Make no excuses.
Rationalize nothing.
Blame no one.
Humble yourself.*
BETH MOORE

*You'll never win the blame game,
so why even bother to play?*
MARIE T. FREEMAN

*Man must cease attributing
his problems to his environment,
and learn again to exercise his will—
his personal responsibility
in the realm of faith and morals.*
ALBERT SCHWEITZER

*Bear with the faults of others as
you would have them bear with yours.*
PHILLIPS BROOKS

MORE FROM GOD'S WORD

Don't let your spirit rush to be angry, for anger abides in the heart of fools.
ECCLESIASTES 7:9 HCSB

All bitterness, anger and wrath, shouting and slander must be removed from you, along with all malice. And be kind and compassionate to one another, forgiving one another, just as God also forgave you in Christ.
EPHESIANS 4:31–32 HCSB

Therefore, laying aside falsehood, speak truth each one of you with his neighbor, for we are members of one another.
EPHESIANS 4:25 NASB

REMEMBER THIS

If you're spending time and energy blaming others for your problems—or if you're focusing too intently on the past—it's time to redirect your thoughts and rearrange your priorities. And while you're at it, remember that you can't win the blame game, so there's no logical reason to play.

A TIMELY TIP

Because blame focuses your mind on the negative aspects of your life, it's an emotional dead end. So instead of looking for somebody to blame, look for something to do, something that helps you build a better future for yourself and your loved ones.

32

FEAR NOT; GOD IS BIGGER THAN YOUR DIFFICULTIES

What the Bible Says

Fear not, for I am with you; be not dismayed, for I am your God. I will strengthen you, yes, I will help you, I will uphold you with My righteous right hand.

Isaiah 41:10 NKJV

As believers in a risen Christ, we can, and should, live courageously. After all, Jesus promises us that He has overcome the world and that He has made a place for us in heaven. So we have nothing to fear in the long term because our Lord will care for us throughout eternity. But what about those short-term, everyday worries that keep us up at night? And what about the life-altering hardships that leave us wondering if we can ever recover? The answer, of course, is that because God cares for us in good times and hard times, we can turn our concerns over to Him in prayer, knowing that all things ultimately work for the good of those who love Him. When we focus upon our fears and our doubts, we may find many reasons to lie awake at night and fret about the uncertainties of the coming day. A better strategy, of course, is to focus not upon our fears, but instead upon our God.

The Lord is as near as your next breath, and He is in control. He offers salvation to all His children, including you. God is your shield and your strength; you are His forever. So don't focus your thoughts upon the fears of the day. Instead, trust God's plan and

His eternal love for you. And remember: God is good, and He has the final word.

MORE THOUGHTS ABOUT OVERCOMING FEAR

Fear is a self-imposed prison that will keep you from becoming what God intends for you to be. You must move against it with the weapons of faith and love.

Rick Warren

A perfect faith would lift us absolutely above fear.

George MacDonald

The presence of fear does not mean you have no faith. Fear visits everyone. But make your fear a visitor and not a resident.

Max Lucado

God shields us from most of the things we fear, but when He chooses not to shield us, He unfailingly allots grace in the measure needed.

Elisabeth Elliot

God's power is great enough for our deepest desperation. You can go on. You can pick up the pieces and start anew. You can face your fears. You can find peace in the rubble. There is healing for your soul.

Suzanne Dale Ezell

It is good to remind ourselves that the will of God comes from the heart of God and that we need not be afraid.

WARREN WIERSBE

MORE FROM GOD'S WORD

Be not afraid, only believe.
MARK 5:36 KJV

But He said to them, "It is I; do not be afraid."
JOHN 6:20 NKJV

Even though I walk through the darkest valley, I will fear no evil, for you are with me; your rod and your staff, they comfort me.
PSALM 23:4 NIV

REMEMBER THIS

Everybody faces obstacles. Don't overestimate the size of yours.

A TIMELY TIP

Are you feeling anxious or fearful? If so, trust God to handle those problems that are simply too big for you to solve. Entrust the future—your future—to the Lord. The two of you, working together, can accomplish great things for His kingdom.

33

SAY NO TO CHRONIC COMPLAINING

What the Bible Says

Be hospitable to one another without complaining.

1 PETER 4:9 HCSB

Because we are imperfect human beings, we often lose sight of our blessings. Ironically, most of us have more blessings than we can count, but we may still find reasons to complain about the minor frustrations of everyday life. To do so, of course, is not only wrong, it is also the pinnacle of shortsightedness and a serious roadblock on the path to spiritual abundance.

Sometimes we give voice to our complaints, and on other occasions, we manage to keep our protestations to ourselves. But even when no one else hears our complaints, God does.

Would you like to feel more comfortable about your circumstances and your life? Then promise yourself that you'll do whatever it takes to ensure that you focus your thoughts on the major blessings you've received, not the minor hardships you must occasionally endure. So the next time you're tempted to complain about the unavoidable frustrations of everyday living, don't do it. Instead, make it a practice to count your blessings, not your inconveniences. It's the truly decent way to live.

MORE THOUGHTS ABOUT SAYING NO TO CHRONIC COMPLAINTS

Don't complain. The more you complain about things, the more things you'll have to complain about.
E. Stanley Jones

Thanksgiving or complaining—these words express two contrasting attitudes of the souls of God's children. The soul that gives thanks can find comfort in everything; the soul that complains can find comfort in nothing.
Hannah Whitall Smith

If we have our eyes upon ourselves, our problems, and our pain, we cannot lift our eyes upward.
Billy Graham

It is always possible to be thankful for what is given rather than to complain about what is not given. One or the other becomes a habit of life.
Elisabeth Elliot

Grumbling and gratitude are, for the child of God, in conflict. Be grateful and you won't grumble. Grumble and you won't be grateful.
Billy Graham

Gratitude is riches. Complaint is poverty.
Doris Day

MORE FROM GOD'S WORD

My dear brothers and sisters, always be willing to listen and slow to speak.
JAMES 1:19 NCV

He who guards his lips guards his life, but he who speaks rashly will come to ruin.
PROVERBS 13:3 NIV

Those who consider themselves religious and yet do not keep a tight rein on their tongues deceive themselves, and their religion is worthless.
JAMES 1:26 NIV

REMEMBER THIS

To experience the full measure of God's blessings, you must give praise and thanks to the Giver. So make it a point to thank God for His blessings many times each day.

A TIMELY TIP

If you feel a personal pity party coming on, slow down and thank your heavenly Father for gifts that are, in truth, too numerous to count. If you fill your heart with gratitude, there's simply no room left for complaints.

34

GOD WANTS YOU TO FORGIVE EVERYBODY, INCLUDING YOURSELF

What the Bible Says

Above all, love each other deeply, because love covers a multitude of sins.
1 Peter 4:8 NIV

Forgiveness isn't a feeling or an emotion or an involuntary reaction. Forgiveness is a choice. When we've been hurt, we can choose to forgive, or not. The decision is ours, as are the consequences.

If you're having trouble forgiving someone, you can be sure of one thing: You haven't prayed about it enough. Constant prayer changes things and it changes you. When you sincerely bow your head and ask Your Creator for help, you'll receive it, but not necessarily at the exact time, or in the exact way, that you asked for it. The Lord always answers our prayers, but He does so in His own way and according to His own plan. Sometimes you'll need to pray long and hard before He responds in a way that you can understand.

If there exists even one person—alive or dead—against whom you hold bitter feelings, it's time to forgive. Or if you are embittered against yourself for some past mistake or shortcoming, it's finally time to forgive yourself and move on. Hatred, bitterness, and regret are not part of God's plan for your life. Forgiveness is.

MORE THOUGHTS ABOUT FORGIVENESS

*Forgiveness is an act of the will,
and the will can function regardless
of the temperature of the heart.*
CORRIE TEN BOOM

*Forgiveness does not change the past,
but it does enlarge the future.*
DAVID JEREMIAH

*Forgiveness is one of the most
beautiful words in the human vocabulary.
How much pain could be avoided if
we all learned the meaning of this word!*
BILLY GRAHAM

*In one bold stroke, forgiveness obliterates
the past and permits us to enter
the land of new beginnings.*
BILLY GRAHAM

Forgiveness is God's command.
MARTIN LUTHER

*Remember that you will never be
spiritually blessed until you forgive.*
NORMAN VINCENT PEALE

MORE FROM GOD'S WORD

*The merciful are blessed,
for they will be shown mercy.*
MATTHEW 5:7 HCSB

*But I say to you, love your enemies
and pray for those who persecute you.*
MATTHEW 5:44 NASB

*And whenever you stand praying,
if you have anything against anyone,
forgive him, so that your Father
in heaven will also forgive
you your wrongdoing.*
MARK 11:25 HCSB

REMEMBER THIS

Forgiveness is its own reward. Bitterness is its own punishment, and bitter thoughts are bad for your spiritual and emotional health. Guard your words and thoughts accordingly.

A TIMELY TIP

If at first you can't forgive, keep trying and keep praying. When it comes to the task of forgiving others, God wants you to be relentless. He wants you to start forgiving now and keep forgiving until it sticks.

35

TOO EDGY?

What the Bible Says

But the fruit of the Spirit is love, joy, peace, longsuffering, kindness, goodness, faithfulness, gentleness, self-control. Against such there is no law.
GALATIANS 5:22–23 NKJV

None of us are perfect, so all of us can, on occasion, be victimized by negativity and anger. As a result, all of us can become irritable from time to time. These feelings should be temporary, not permanent fixtures of our individual psychological landscapes. So if you're chronically angry, irritable, or bitter, you need a spiritual makeover.

The path to spiritual maturity unfolds day by day. Each day offers the opportunity to worship God, to ignore God, or to rebel against God. When we worship Him with our prayers, our words, our thoughts, and our actions, we are blessed by the richness of our relationship with the Father. But if we ignore God altogether or intentionally rebel against His commandments, we rob ourselves of His blessings.

If we study God's Word, if we obey His commandments, and if we live in the center of His will, we will not be angry, irritable, or bitter. Instead, we will be growing Christians, and that's exactly what the Lord wants for our lives.

Many of life's most important lessons are painful to learn, but spiritual growth need not take place only in times of adversity. We must seek to grow in our knowledge and love of the Lord in every season of life. Thankfully, God always stands at the door; whenever we are ready to reach out to Him, He will answer. In those quiet moments when we open our hearts to the Father, the One who made us keeps remaking us. He gives us direction, perspective, wisdom, and peace. And the appropriate moment to accept those spiritual gifts is always the present one.

MORE THOUGHTS ABOUT BEING GRATEFUL, NOT EDGY

*For every minute you remain angry,
you give up sixty seconds of peace of mind.*
RALPH WALDO EMERSON

Keep cool; anger is not an argument.
DANIEL WEBSTER

*Anger and bitterness—whatever the cause—
only end up hurting us.
Turn that anger over to Christ.*
BILLY GRAHAM

*In a controversy, the instant we
feel anger we have already ceased
striving for the truth and have
begun striving for ourselves.*
THOMAS CARLYLE

*Have a heart that never hardens, and a temper
that never fires, and a touch that never hurts.*
CHARLES DICKENS

We must guard against allowing anger to drag us into sin.
JOYCE MEYER

MORE FROM GOD'S WORD

A gentle answer turns away wrath, but a harsh word stirs up anger.
PROVERBS 15:1 NIV

A person's insight gives him patience, and his virtue is to overlook an offense.
PROVERBS 19:11 HCSB

REMEMBER THIS

Sometimes peace can be a scarce commodity in a noisy, complicated, twenty-first-century world. But God's peace is always available when you turn everything over to Him.

A TIMELY TIP

Because all of us are human, we all experience occasional bouts of irritability. But intense, unrelenting irritability can be a warning sign of an underlying psychological or physiological condition that can be treated with therapy or medication or both. So if you or someone you love is seriously, chronically, dangerously ill-tempered, don't suffer in silence. Instead, talk things over with someone you trust. And if the symptoms are serious, don't hesitate to seek professional guidance before the emotional roller coaster runs off the tracks.

36

IF YOU'RE STARTING OVER

What the Bible Says

Then the One seated on the throne said, "Look! I am making everything new."
REVELATION 21:5 HCSB

If you've recently extricated yourself from a difficult situation—or if you've experienced the end of an important relationship—you may feel like you're entering a new phase of life. If so, congratulations. Your fresh start is an occasion to be celebrated. God has a perfect plan for your life, and He has the power to make all things new. As you think about your future—and as you consider the countless opportunities that will be woven into the fabric of the days ahead—be sure to include God in your plans. When you do, He will guide your steps and light your path.

Perhaps you desire to change the direction of your life, or perhaps you're determined to make major modifications in the way you live or the way you think. If so, you and the Lord, working together, can do it. But don't expect change to be easy or instant. God expects you to do your fair share of the work, and that's as it should be.

If you're going through a spiritual growth spurt, don't be surprised if you experience a few spiritual growing pains. Why? Because real transformation begins on the inside and works its way out from there. And sometimes the "working out" process can be painful. Lasting change doesn't occur "out there"; it occurs "in here." It occurs, not in the shifting sands of your own particular circumstances, but in the quiet depths of your own obedient heart. So if you're in search of a new beginning or, for that matter, a new you, don't expect changing circumstances to miraculously transform you into the person you want to become. Transformation starts with God, and it starts in the silent center of a humble human heart—like yours.

MORE THOUGHTS ABOUT STARTING OVER

Each day you must say to yourself, "Today I am going to begin."
JEAN PIERRE DE CAUSSADE

The best preparation for the future is the present well seen to, and the last duty done.
GEORGE MACDONALD

People aren't born to be failures. Those who quietly persevere always have a chance.
JIMMY STEWART

What saves a man is to take a step. Then another step.
C. S. LEWIS

Are you in earnest? Seize this very minute. what you can do, or dream you can do, begin it. Boldness has genius, power, and magic in it.
JOHANN WOLFGANG VON GOETHE

MORE FROM GOD'S WORD

*"For I know the plans I have for you"—
this is the Lord's declaration—
"plans for your welfare, not for disaster,
to give you a future and a hope."*

JEREMIAH 29:11 HCSB

*Your old sinful self has died, and your
new life is kept with Christ in God.*

COLOSSIANS 3:3 NCV

*There is one thing I always do. Forgetting
the past and straining toward what is ahead,
I keep trying to reach the goal
and get the prize for which God called me.*

PHILIPPIANS 3:13–14 NCV

REMEMBER THIS

When you are tested, don't quit at the first sign of trouble. Instead, call upon God. He can give you the strength to persevere, and that's exactly what you should ask Him to do.

A TIMELY TIP

If you're graduating into a new phase of life, be sure to make God your partner. If you do, He'll help carry your burdens, and He'll help you focus on the opportunities of the future, not the losses of the past.

37

WHEN YOU'RE SUFFERING, GOD CAN HEAL YOU

What the Bible Says

And the God of all grace, who called you to his eternal glory in Christ, after you have suffered a little while, will himself restore you and make you strong, firm and steadfast.

1 PETER 5:10 NIV

All of us face times of adversity. When we face the inevitable difficulties of life here on earth, we should seek help from family, from friends, and from God, but not necessarily in that order. Barbara Johnson wrote, "There is no way around suffering. We have to go through it to get to the other side." And the best way "to get to the other side" of suffering is to get there with God. When we turn open hearts to Him in heartfelt prayer, He will answer—in His own time and according to His own plan—and He will heal us. And while we are waiting for God's plans to unfold and for His healing touch to restore us, we can be comforted in the knowledge that our Creator can overcome any obstacle, even if we cannot.

The psalmist wrote, "Weeping may endure for a night, but joy comes in the morning" (Psalm 30:5 NKJV). But when we are suffering, the morning may seem very far away. It is not. God promises that He is "near to those who have a broken heart" (Psalm 34:18).

So even if you've experienced a heartbreaking disappointment or a life-altering loss, don't allow pain and regret to dominate your life. As you move through and beyond your suffering, you can—and should—train yourself to think less about your pain and more about God's love. Focus your mind on Him, and let your sorrows fend for themselves.

MORE THOUGHTS ABOUT GOD'S COMFORT WHEN WE SUFFER

God is sufficient for all our needs, for every problem, for every difficulty, for every broken heart, for every human sorrow.
PETER MARSHALL

You don't have to be alone in your hurt! Comfort is yours. Joy is an option. And it's all been made possible by your Savior.
JONI EARECKSON TADA

The promises of God's Word sustain us in our suffering, and we know Jesus sympathizes and empathizes with us in our darkest hour.
BILL BRIGHT

Suffering is never for nothing. It is that you and I might be conformed to the image of Christ.
ELISABETH ELLIOT

God whispers to us in our pleasures, speaks in our conscience, but shouts in our pains: it is His megaphone to rouse a deaf world.
C. S. LEWIS

MORE FROM GOD'S WORD

*I have heard your prayer;
I have seen your tears. Look, I will heal you.*
2 Kings 20:5 HCSB

I have told you these things so that in Me you may have peace. You will have suffering in this world. Be courageous! I have conquered the world.
John 16:33 HCSB

In my distress I called upon the Lord, and cried unto my God: he heard my voice.
Psalm 18:6 KJV

REMEMBER THIS

Tough times are simply opportunities to trust God completely and to find strength in Him. And remember that hard times can also be times of intense personal growth.

A TIMELY TIP

All of us must, from time to time, endure unfortunate circumstances that test our faith. No man or woman, no matter how righteous, is exempt. Christians, however, face their suffering with the ultimate armor: God's promises. The Lord has the power to heal us if we welcome Him into our hearts.

38

TRUST GOD'S WISDOM

WHAT THE BIBLE SAYS

For the Lord gives wisdom; from His mouth come knowledge and understanding.

Proverbs 2:6 HCSB

Real wisdom doesn't come from talk radio, reality TV, the sports page, the evening news, or from a Facebook page. In fact, searching for genuine nuggets of wisdom in the endless stream of modern-day media messages is like panning for gold without a pan, only harder. Why? Because real wisdom doesn't come from the world; it comes from the Lord . . . and it's up to you to ask Him for it. Jesus made it clear to His disciples that they should petition God to meet their needs (Matthew 7:7–8). So should you.

Genuine, heartfelt prayer produces powerful changes in you and in your world. When you lift your heart to God, you open yourself to a never-ending source of divine wisdom and infinite love. Yet too many folks are too timid or pessimistic to ask the Lord for help. Please don't count yourself among their number.

God will give you wisdom if you ask Him. So ask. Ask Him to meet the needs of your day. Ask Him to lead you, to protect you, to guide you, and to correct you. Then trust the answers He gives.

MORE THOUGHTS ABOUT GOD'S WISDOM

To know the will of God is the highest of all wisdom.

Billy Graham

*True wisdom is marked by willingness to listen
and a sense of knowing when to yield.*
ELIZABETH GEORGE

MORE FROM GOD'S WORD

*Who among you is wise and understanding?
Let him show by his good behavior
his deeds in the gentleness of wisdom.*
JAMES 3:13 NASB

*But the wisdom that is from above is first pure,
then peaceable, gentle, willing to yield,
full of mercy and good fruits,
without partiality and without hypocrisy.*
JAMES 3:17 NKJV

*But if any of you lacks wisdom, let him ask of God,
who gives to all generously and without reproach,
and it will be given to him.*
JAMES 1:5 NASB

REMEMBER THIS

If you want God's guidance, ask for it. When you pray for guidance, the Lord will give it.

A TIMELY TIP

Need wisdom? God's got it and He wants you to acquire it. If you want the same thing, then study His Word, obey His teachings, follow as closely as you can in the footsteps of His Son, and associate with people who do likewise.

39

STAY FOCUSED ON GOD'S GIFT OF ETERNAL LIFE

What the Bible Says

For God so loved the world, that he gave his only begotten Son, that whosoever believeth in him should not perish, but have everlasting life.

JOHN 3:16 KJV

Your life here on earth is merely preparation for a far different life to come: the eternal life that God promises to those who welcome His Son into their hearts. As a mere mortal, your vision for the future is finite, but the Lord's vision is not burdened by such limitations; His plans extend throughout all eternity. Thus, God's plans for you are not limited to the ups and downs of everyday life. Your heavenly Father has bigger things in mind, *much* bigger things.

How marvelous it is that God became a man and walked among us. Had He not chosen to do so, we might feel removed from a distant Creator. But ours is not a distant God. Ours is a God who understands—far better than we ever could—the essence of what it means to be human. He understands our hopes, our fears, our anxieties, and our temptations. He understands what it means to be angry and what it costs to forgive. He knows the heart, the conscience, the soul, and the emotions of every person who has ever lived, including you.

As you struggle with the inevitable hardships and occasional disappointments of everyday life, remember that God has invited you to accept His abundance not only for today but also for all eternity. So keep things in perspective. Although you will inevitably encounter occasional defeats in this world, you'll have all eternity to celebrate the ultimate victory in the next.

MORE THOUGHTS ABOUT ETERNAL LIFE

*Death is not a journey into an unknown land;
it is a voyage home. We are going,
not to a strange country but to our Father's house.*
JOHN RUSKIN

*At most, you will live a hundred years on earth,
but you will spend forever in eternity.*
RICK WARREN

*Death is not the end of life;
it is only the gateway to eternity.*
BILLY GRAHAM

*Jesus became mortal to give you immortality;
and today, through Him, you can be free.*
DAVID JEREMIAH

*Everything that is joined to the immortal Head
will share His immortality.*
C. S. LEWIS

You need to think more about eternity and not less.
RICK WARREN

MORE FROM GOD'S WORD

The last enemy that will be destroyed is death.
1 Corinthians 15:26 NKJV

I assure you: Anyone who hears My word and believes Him who sent Me has eternal life and will not come under judgment, but has passed from death to life.
John 5:24 HCSB

For the wages of sin is death, but the gift of God is eternal life in Christ Jesus our Lord.
Romans 6:23 NIV

REMEMBER THIS

If you have already welcomed Christ into your heart as your personal Savior, then you are safe. If you're still sitting on the fence, the time to accept Him is this very moment.

A TIMELY TIP

Once you've welcomed Christ into your heart, you have an important story to tell: yours. So don't be hesitant to share your personal testimony with the world.

COMMON MOOD AND ANXIETY DISORDERS

Tough times can be stressful. Very stressful. And when our stress levels are increased, we are at higher risk of experiencing a mood or anxiety disorder. These disorders can be serious, life-threatening conditions, but they're also highly treatable, so it's important to identify them early and to seek treatment expeditiously.

A mood disorder is a mental health condition that has an adverse effect on a person's emotional state. The two most common mood disorders are depression and bipolar disorder. Both of these conditions are further divided into subcategories based, in part, on the severity and duration of the person's symptoms.

An anxiety disorder is a condition that causes exaggerated emotions to interfere with a person's ability to lead a normal life. All of us feel anxious from time to time, but a person who experiences an anxiety disorder is faced with overwhelming, debilitating feelings of fear, dread, or panic. Obsessive behaviors—characterized by recurrent, unwanted thoughts (obsessions) or undesirable repetitive behaviors (compulsions)—are also considered to be anxiety-related conditions.

Mood and anxiety disorders are quite common. The National Institute of Mental Health (NIMH) estimates that almost 10 percent of US adults will experience a mood disorder during a given year and that over 20 percent of adults will experience a mood disorder sometime during their lifetime.

Anxiety disorders are even more common than mood disorders. In fact, the NIMH calls anxiety disorders "the most common mental health concern in the United States." They estimate that currently about 40 million adults (almost 20 percent of the adult population) suffer from some type of anxiety-related condition.

Common anxiety disorders include, but are not limited to: generalized anxiety disorder, obsessive-compulsive disorder, panic disorder, post-traumatic stress disorder, and social anxiety disorder.

Both mood and anxiety disorders tend to run in families, which means that they can be inherited from one or both parents. Additionally, environmental factors—such as a traumatic event, a serious illness, or a significant life-changing situation—can be causal factors.

Clearly mood and anxiety disorders pose serious problems for individual sufferers and for the loved ones who care about them. Thankfully, these disorders are, in most cases, readily treatable with therapy or medication or a combination of the two, combined with self-care.

The following descriptions provide a brief introduction to the above-mentioned disorders. Should you need to learn more, detailed information is readily available. And if you suspect that you or someone you care about may be impacted by one of these disorders, or by a mental illness not mentioned here, don't wait to seek treatment. Mental health problems can evolve into serious, debilitating, life-threatening conditions. So it's always better to seek professional guidance sooner rather than later.

The Most Common Mood Disorders

Major Depression (also known as Major Depressive Disorder or Clinical Depression): Major depression is a common, serious mood disorder. It causes severe symptoms that affect how one feels, thinks, and manages daily activities such as sleeping, eating, or working. To be diagnosed with depression, symptoms must be present for at least two weeks. Symptoms include, but are not limited to:

- Feelings of sadness, hopeless, or despondency

- Feelings of guilt, worthlessness, or helplessness
- Difficulty sleeping, early-morning awakening, or oversleeping
- Having noticeably less interest in usual pleasurable activities
- Decreased energy level
- Appetite or weight changes
- Feeling that life no longer has meaning
- Irritability
- Moving or talking more slowly
- Feeling restless or having trouble sitting still
- Difficulty concentrating, remembering, or making decisions
- Thoughts of death or suicide, or suicide attempts
- Aches or pains, headaches, cramps, or digestive problems that have no clear physical cause

Bipolar Disorder (also known as Manic-Depressive Disorder): According to NIMH, bipolar disorder is "a brain disorder that causes unusual shifts in mood, energy, activity levels, and the ability to carry out day-to-day tasks." People suffering with this condition experience episodes of depression alternating with periods of mania.

There are four basic types of bipolar disorder, all of which involve demonstrable changes in mood, energy, and activity levels. These moods vacillate between periods of extreme energy and/or irritability (known as manic episodes) followed by periods of extreme sadness, hopelessness, or despair (known as depressive episodes). According to NIMH, people experiencing manic episodes may exhibit some or most of the following symptoms:

- Feeling very "up," "high," or elated
- Feeling extremely energetic
- Increased activity levels

- Feeling jumpy or "wired"
- Trouble falling asleep or staying asleep
- Exhibiting pressured speech patterns, such as talking faster than normal
- Feeling agitated, irritable, or "touchy"
- Racing thoughts
- Attempting to do many things at once

According to NIMH, bipolar patients experiencing depressive episodes may exhibit some or most of the following symptoms:

- Feeling very sad, down, empty, or hopeless
- Having very little energy
- Exhibiting decreased activity levels
- Trouble sleeping (either too little sleep or too much)
- Feeling unable to enjoy anything
- Feeling worried and empty
- Trouble concentrating
- Forgetfulness
- Eating too much or too little
- Feeling tired or "slowed down"
- Thinking about death or suicide

OTHER COMMON MOOD DISORDERS

Persistent Depressive Disorder (also known as Dysthymia): This is a chronic, low-grade mood disorder in which symptoms of depression or irritability last for at least two years. A person diagnosed with persistent depressive disorder may experience episodes of major depression along with periods of less severe symptoms. But for a diagnosis of persistent depressive disorder, the depressive symptoms—both major symptoms and less severe ones—must last, in total, for at least two years.

Postpartum Depression: Many women become mildly depressed or anxious after the birth of a child. These symptoms, if they occur at all, typically clear up within two weeks after delivery. Postpartum depression is a much more serious condition. Women with postpartum depression experience a full-blown major depression after delivery. Feelings of extreme sadness, anxiety, and exhaustion are common, thus making it difficult for mothers to care for themselves and for their babies.

Seasonal Affective Disorder (SAD): This is a form of depression that occurs during certain seasons of the year. Typically SAD begins in the late autumn or early winter and lasts until spring or summer. Less commonly, SAD episodes may begin during the late spring or summer. Symptoms of winter seasonal affective disorder often resemble those of major depression.

THE MOST COMMON ANXIETY DISORDERS

Generalized Anxiety Disorder (GAD): This condition is characterized by chronic anxiety, by exaggerated worry, tension, and apprehension even when there is no discernable cause for those feelings.

GAD, which often begins in the teen years or early adulthood, develops slowly. According to NIMH, symptoms of GAD include:

- Being excessively worried about everyday things
- Having trouble controlling worries or feelings of nervousness
- Knowing that one's worries are exaggerated and excessive
- Feeling restless; having trouble relaxing
- Difficulty concentrating
- Easily startled
- Having trouble falling asleep or staying asleep
- Feeling tired most or all the time

- Experiencing physical symptoms, such as headaches, muscle aches, stomach aches, or unexplained pains
- Difficulty swallowing
- Experiencing twitches or tremors
- Being irritable or feeling "on edge"
- Sweating profusely, feeling lightheaded or out of breath

Children and teens with GAD often worry excessively about:

- Performances in school, sports, or other public activities
- Catastrophes such as earthquakes or wars

Adults with GAD are often highly nervous about everyday circumstances, such as:

- Job security or performance
- Health
- Finances
- The health and well-being of their children
- Being late
- Completing household chores and other responsibilities

Post-traumatic Stress Disorder (PTSD): This disorder develops in some people who have either experienced or witnessed a terrifying, life-threatening, or life-altering event. PTSD symptoms may start within one month of the traumatic event, but for many individuals, symptoms may not appear until years later. These symptoms create significant problems in social settings, work-related environments, and relationships. PTSD symptoms are generally grouped into four categories: intrusive memories, avoidance, negative changes in thinking and mood, and changes in physical and emotional reactions.

Obsessive-Compulsive Disorder (OCD): This anxiety disorder is characterized by recurrent, unwanted thoughts (obsessions) and/or repetitive behaviors (compulsions). Repetitive behaviors such as hand washing, counting, checking, or cleaning are often performed with the hope of preventing obsessive thoughts or making those thoughts go away. Performing these rituals, however, provides only temporary relief. Not performing the aforementioned repetitive behaviors causes psychological discomfort and a marked increase in anxiety.

Panic Disorder: This anxiety disorder is characterized by unexpected and repeated episodes of intense fear (panic attacks) accompanied by physical and psychological symptoms that include:

- Sudden and repeated panic attacks that result in overwhelming feelings of anxiety and fear
- The feeling of being out of control
- The fear of death or impending doom during a panic attack
- Physical symptoms during a panic attack, such as a pounding or racing heart, sweating, chills, trembling, breathing problems, weakness or dizziness, tingly or numb hands, chest pain, stomach pain, or nausea
- An intense worry about when the next panic attack will occur
- A fear or avoidance of places where panic attacks have occurred in the past

Social Anxiety Disorder (also knowns as Social Phobia): This disorder is characterized by excessive self-consciousness and overwhelming anxiety resulting from social or performance situations in which the person is exposed to unfamiliar people or to possible scrutiny by others. A person with social phobia fears that he or she may act in a way—or may display anxiety-related symptoms—that will cause embarrassment or humiliation. In extreme cases, the phobia may be so broad that the sufferer experiences symptoms almost anytime he or she interacts with other people.

A FINAL NOTE

For previous generations, mental illness was often spoken about in whispers. For many sufferers and their families, emotional disorders were a source of embarrassment or shame, but thankfully, this is no longer the case. Today, mental health is a top-of-mind priority for medical professionals who are keenly aware of countless studies that clearly demonstrate that most mental disorders have both medical as well as psychological origins. As such, most emotional disorders are now readily treatable. Thanks to advances in medical science, healing is available through counseling, through medication, or through a combination of the two.

If you suspect that you—or someone you care about—may be experiencing a mood disorder, an anxiety disorder, or any other psychiatric condition, don't hesitate to seek professional help. To fully experience God's abundance, you need to be spiritually and emotionally healthy. If mental health professionals can help you achieve the emotional stability you need to fully experience God's abundance here on earth, you should consider your treatment to be part of God's plan for your life.